AF552388

DIANA GUEST
STONECARVER

DIANA GUEST
STONECARVER

Photographs by
Christian Odasso

Comments by
Diana Guest, Raymond Charmet,
Marion Pike, and Jim Harrison

CLARK CITY PRESS
LIVINGSTON, MONTANA

 PRINTED IN THE UNITED STATES OF AMERICA.
GUEST, DIANA.
DIANA GUEST, STONECARVER / ESSAYS BY DIANA GUEST . . . [ET AL.] :
PHOTOGRAPHS BY CHRISTIAN ODASSO.
P. CM.
INCLUDES INDEX.
ISBN 0-944439-16-0 : $60.00
1. GUEST, DIANA — THEMES, MOTIVES. I. TITLE.
NB497.G84A4 1992
730'.92 — DC20 92-21487
CIP

Clark City Press
109 WEST CALLENDER
LIVINGSTON, MONTANA 59047

To Saint Francis of Assisi,
protector of all animals,
and to my brothers Winston and Raymond,
who shared my love of nature.

CONTENTS

Preface by Diana Guest 1

Comments by

Raymond Charmet 7

Marion Pike 9

Jim Harrison 11

Plates

1953–1965 13

1965–1978 45

1978–1992 79

List of Plates 149

Exhibitions 151

He prayeth well who loveth well
Both man and bird and beast.

SAMUEL TAYLOR COLERIDGE

I was born and brought up in the country in England. My parents, Amy Phipps and Frederick Guest, met in India and married a year later in London. They settled in a beautiful Queen Anne house near Oakham named Burley on the Hill. It was made of grey stone and stood on a high hill overlooking a forest of ancient trees and a series of fish ponds. There were all sorts of animals, from polo ponies to sheep. I had a Shetland pony named Togo to ride and a mare named Milk Maid to take us to the village every day in a tub-shaped pony cart. The woods were filled with bluebells and ferns, and my brothers and I crawled down the rabbit paths. On moonlit nights, I used to sit on my window ledge and watch the rabbits play on the lawn below. Near the chapel attached to the house, there was a dog cemetery. Though I had my brothers, I was often lonely and greatly preferred being with my dog or on my horse than with my rather strict nurses or governess. I think this is why I instinctively carve animals and birds.

I saw stranger creatures at our farm north of Nairobi, at the foot of Mount Kenya. A stream ran near the main house, and waterbuck, tommy deer, wild pigs, impala and sometimes rhinos drank from it. The buffalo always stayed a few miles away on the side of the mountain, near what is now Treetops. When setting camp on safari, sometimes at altitudes as high as 15,000 feet, the first thing we always did was put out water for the bees, dying of thirst, lest they sting us for the sake of our blood. My father and I both had planes, De Haviland Moths, and we cleared a landing strip on the farm. I often had to drive the deer away in order to take off. My father and I made many trips up and down the Nile and visited the tombs and temples and the snake charmers of Cairo. I still hear the music of their pipes and see the swaying cobras.

It was a great advantage for me to have been brought up surrounded by beauty and beautiful things; these trained my eye. It distresses me to see so many ugly things exhibited in museums these days. A museum should be an inspiration to create beauty. One of the reasons I think I chose sculpture as a form of expression is that, when I was young, I admired the work of a very talented woman named Claire Sheridan. She did the heads of many of the people around me, including my father; Winston Churchill; and F. E. Smith, Lord Birkenhead. Art seems to run in the family. My mother would certainly have been an architect had she lived today. She had a wonderful eye for proportion and beauty and especially enjoyed the temples and sculpture of Greece. My cousin Winston Churchill, besides his great statesmanship, was a fine writer and a truly talented painter. His daughter, Mary Soames, inherited his writing abilities and his granddaughter, Edwina Sandys, is a sculptor of merit. My son is a writer and one of my granddaughters is an architect and designer. I am grateful to my forebears for having passed down to me a desire to express beauty, as well as the means to live amongst it.

In Mary Soames' *Winston Churchill: His Life as a Painter*, she quotes: "To have reached the age of forty, without ever handling a brush or fiddling with a pencil, to have regarded with a mature eye, the painting of pictures of any kind as a mystery, to have stood agape before the chalk of the pavement artist and then suddenly to find oneself plunged in the middle of a new and intense form of interest and action with paints and not to be discouraged by the results, is an astonishing and enriching experience." This is how I felt when I had the temerity to grasp a hammer and chisel and attack a beautiful virgin block of marble for the first time.

It was not until I had learned to fly, danced all night, traveled the world over and had two husbands and three children that I had the time and opportunity to learn to carve stone. When my children reached school age, I was living in Paris, and I asked my architect friends if they knew of a teacher. They suggested Salomé Vernard.

Her studio was located in the 14th Arrondissement in an alley off the Avenue Jean Moulin. Salomé was very bohemian, with red hair and green eyes that saw everything. We soon became good friends, and remained so until her death.

On my first day, I was given a hammer and point and told how to stand, legs a little apart, wrist fairly relaxed, to work at shoulder height. I was presented with a rough block of marble of no particular shape and was shown which three points to strike—the first two loosen or *brisée* the stone, and the third stroke makes it jump or *sauté*. Right from the start, you must learn to listen to your stroke on the stone, as that will tell you if there is a fault or *faille* in your stone (onyx is particularly prone to splitting).

When I graduated to working alone, I always started by drawing my figure on the stone with a black charcoal pencil, beginning with the head or beak, which I kept deliberately massive until the end. The mysteries unfold very gradually; only when you have everything in place do you use a rasp for smoothing the surface, and once you have started on a certain subject, you cannot and must not change your subject or pose. At the end of every day you must leave your work looking wholesome and never grotesque. When you see it in the morning, it will be a pleasant surprise and your respect for such a noble material will sustain you. It should be pure, strong and simple, as the Greeks and Egyptians interpreted their sculpture, each in their own style. The flow of curves and forms should so please the eye that the desire to touch is irresistible, and hands reach out to caress the cool sculpture, as if it were the cheek of a child or the muzzle of a horse.

My daughter Lorraine, aged ten, was my first model for a portrait, and I was lucky that she was so pretty and patient. She sat on a pedestal with a book, hour after hour, while Salome and I wandered around her, taking measurements, observing the tilt of her nose, the distance between her eyes and the curve of her lips. The next summer, my son Guy was the martyr, but he posed very well and patiently.

Soon after, I found my own studio, near Val de Grace Hospital. I walked through an open doorway into an old building and there beyond was a small house in the process of being rebuilt. It had four large French windows and a door and a roof, and that appeared to be all. The owner was willing to sell, so it became mine.

It was fun organizing the place. The four windows gave me plenty of light, and I put a round skylight in the ceiling of the main room. Being small, the house was soon liveable, and I frequented the flea market for furniture. I planted a catalpa tree and Virginia creeper for the walls. The small courtyard was very agreeable, and allowed me to work outside.

When I was ready to get back to work, I knew at once that I wanted to carve a toad. I have been partial to them since childhood, when I used to pick one up and carry it about. One day I forgot to release my toad and produced it, to my nanny's horror, at table.

I bought a nice onyx block and enjoyed remembering my toad. First I removed all the rough outside layers, so that I could see the stone properly, and then I drew the form I remembered, starting with the large eyes and working down. I placed one hand on his heart, and soon he became my *Amorous Toad*.

I enjoy carving many kinds of stones, each different in texture, each inspiring a different subject and interpretation. My *Grand Duc* is of majestic granite, almost metallic in color; he would hypnotize his prey with the glare of his steely eyes. Greek marble is flesh-colored and invites the artist to carve the human figure in all its subtle, sensuous forms. I have carved many of my animals and birds in a faintly grey marble, which seems to suit them, but have avoided dead white marble as being too cold and austere for my vibrant subjects. I've chosen white alabaster for my flowers and have occasionally been tempted by pink and red, risking the decorative. Soapstone, which is delicate to carve, seems to suit my reptiles and fish. Bronze is very demanding of perfection and sometimes one is disappointed by the result, but as I seldom sell a stone piece, I have many of my birds and animals cast in bronze so that people may buy my work; the proceeds go to animal charities.

For *Cardinal in Flight*, I chose a pink marble from Portugal; my *Giant Snail* is white alabaster, which lets one imagine the slippery path he leaves behind him on each voyage of exploration. I have carved a butterfly of translucent red alabaster that shines like a jewel. For *Europa*, I chose a large pale orange onyx block that contains both the woman and the bull harmoniously.

As time went by and my work progressed, it became necessary to find more stones to carve. Salome and I traveled to Florence, where she was careful to show me the work of the Etruscans and Greeks first, before exposing me to the sculpture of Michelangelo, da Vinci and Donatello. In Rome, I saw St. Peter's, the Vatican and the Coliseum before we traveled to Carrara, the quarry Michelangelo used, and I found a large surface for my *Fallen Horse*. There was great excitement when the block arrived in Paris months later and again in two years when the finished sculpture was lowered to its final resting place in front of the Moulin in Normandy.

We traveled from Carrara to Tarquina to see the Etruscan tombs with their ribald frescoes, and then on to Volterra, near Sienna, set high on a mountain of alabaster. I examined each block carefully, bought twenty, and had them transported to Paris. The purity of the translucent stone and the fullness of the flowers I intended to carve suited each other to perfection. When the blocks arrived months later, I studied each to determine what flower it contained.

These flowers are not the timid ones that blush unseen but express the voluptuousness and exoticism of the tropics. The forms are rich and vibrant with a lust for living. Each flower is languid and sensual, without innocence. The anthurium's stamen is the provocative symbol of sex; the chalice of the lotus tempts with its purity; and the poppy dreams of oblivion.

Some of the flowers I have pushed to the extreme limit of refinement that only alabaster permits. Others are left heavy, acquiescent. My garden is an interpretation of nature's most erotic creations. Enlarged to the monumental, each flower displays its own beauty, its own original design, the rhythm of life—temptation— its ultimate expression. I cultivate my flowers in the sun and under the moon. They are bathed in the light of seduction.

In the summer I work at the Moulin in Normandy, on the grounds of the estate where I raised my children. The Moulin was built as a paper mill, worked by a small waterfall. It lies on an island with the Avre on one side and the Eure on another. Jacques Balsans owned the property before we did, and Churchill painted there often. Because I live on two continents, I am separated from my work sometimes as long as six months, unless I decide to have the sculptures packed and sent to Florida. I see those I leave behind with a fresh eye on my return, and sometimes see the solution to a problem I had wrestled with months before.

I have exhibited in Paris, New York, Switzerland, Palm Beach, Istanbul and London. My sculpture has also been shown at Westbury Gardens, where I spent much of my childhood, with my aunt and uncle and their five children, having treasure hunts and gymkhanas, Fourth of July parties and polo matches. I had always dreamed of showing my flowers at the Phipps Conservatory in Pittsburgh, which was founded by my grandfather. In 1987 this dream became a reality when I placed my work among the tropical ferns and plants. Three years later, my garden—including some insects, a bird or two, a butterfly and a toad—was exhibited for six months at the Brooklyn Botanic Garden.

It is strange that some men and women are driven to use their hands, some to play the piano, some to paint or carve or embroider. William Blake wrote, "Tools are made, but born are hands." Why should this be, but to create beauty? The individual born with this irresistible urge is only happy when at work. Carving is a strange passion, most demanding for someone who is, by nature, active. One stands for hours—years in fact—often with no model but a simple photograph or memory impressed on the inner eye. Music blocks out the dull humdrum of daily details and allows me to enjoy the garden of my mind's eye or the physical one in front of me, the border I planted in front of the studio window at the Moulin in Normandy.

My family crest is a swan's head with two feathers, perhaps one of the reasons why I have raised and admired swans and feel an affinity with them. Each year when I return to the Moulin, they glide up to the house to greet me and to show me their young. They know my voice, and I feed them bread before they float away. I want very much to carve my own version of Leda and the Swan; I see clearly how I would like it to be, but I must first finish a large unicorn that is well advanced in Paris. I see the swan's wings enveloping Leda, and his head resting on her shoulders.

I would leave beauty behind me.

DIANA GUEST

1992

Of all the arts, sculpture is the last to have been conquered by women. For thousands of years, men alone practiced the difficult craft of carving stone and wood and shaping bronze; in this century, however, women have imposed their presence on this art. Diana Guest joins a list that includes Germaine Richier, Jane Poupelet and Berthe Marine.

Diana Guest acquired a mastery of her art long before she decided to show her work in public. Creating exhibits has been less important to her than continuing to travel to the wilderness that inspires her work. Her main theme is nature: not tame or captured animal life, but animals living wild and free.

This is clearly translated in her pure forms and direct approach, which combines her vision of art and her personal character. For years, she has carved directly in stone. The work is subtle and the lines true. The toad with his hand on his heart bows to his love; the round marble pigeon appears the essence of peace; the owl in flight glides over trees; the swordfish seems to swim without effort; the arched, mating fish could be dancers. All are visions of an artist who understands and interprets the speechless language of nature. And whenever Guest casts her eye on man, the same elementary view of life emerges—life as man and beast shared it a million years ago.

The sculptures of Diana Guest are conceived and executed with loving insight and portray a calling of the heart, a call that cannot be denied or resisted.

RAYMOND CHARMET

When one sees the sculpture of Diana Guest for the first time, one is struck by the beauty of the form. She transfers the delicate sensibility of her hands into alabaster, stone and marble, the hardest of materials.

As a painter, I am particularly moved by her technique. Without touching the pieces, one can feel the dew on the translucent alabaster flowers or the strong muscles of the stone animals. But her animals and flowers, with their architectonic quality and voluminous planes, transcend reality and become poetic expression.

Diana Guest is a force of nature, both in herself and in her work. In this era of spikes, squares, cubes and twisted and disjointed materials, it is a delight to see a sculptor who has an empathy and love of nature. To view her work is an emotional and rewarding experience.

MARION PIKE

Twenty years ago or so I stopped in France in late October after a longish trip to the Soviet Union. I left Leningrad in a soul- humbling blizzard, the ferocity of which caused our plane to pirouette on the runway, and landed at Bourget, where I immediately kissed the ground on one of those sun-blasted late autumn days that remind us of their own glorious selves. The next morning I drove with Diana Guest's son, and my friend, Guy de la Valdene, out to her five-hundred-year-old home and horse farm in Normandy, entering a world far stranger to me than Leningrad.

It did not occur to me until I left ten days later that I was leaving a heraldic world where an artist's work resonated the deep past with improbable vividness. Diana's sculpted swans, owls, hawks and horses emerged there and belonged to the soul of the landscape (if you do not believe the land has a soul, look at land that has lost it). It was a reality with a distant but direct relationship to the one we know from tapestries, a reality that emerges from bestiaries written when animals held far more significance than as fodder for environmental squabbles, animals that retained a sacred position in our lives in contrast to something we merely use, take advantage of, that cannot be allowed to exist by and for themselves, or are indulged only if their habitat is not useful to us. One loved them, ate them, chased them, created myths from them—they were not ideas but fellow creatures who shared our joys and dooms.

After so many years I came to know and understand Diana's work more closely, the unmeasurable grace by which she returns the animal its name which had grown meaningless by misuse. Sculpture, like poetry, painting and music, keeps our waning gods alive, restores their youth. Her sculpture is nearly Native American in its simplicity, stopping the world for a moment, as all good art does. Her animals have been given back their "otherness" and are no longer glyphs for our ideas about them. In her work she reaches into this "otherness" and brings it back to us, life forms that we only comprehend in rarest moments, as John Muir did his beloved bears: "Bears are made of the same dust as we and breathe the same winds and drink the same waters, his life not long, not short, knows no beginning, no ending, to him life unstinted, unplanned, is above the accident of time, and his years, markless, boundless, equal eternity."

JIM HARRISON

1953–1965

1 Grand Duc, *granite*

2 Amorous Toad, *onyx*

3 Grand Duc, *granite*

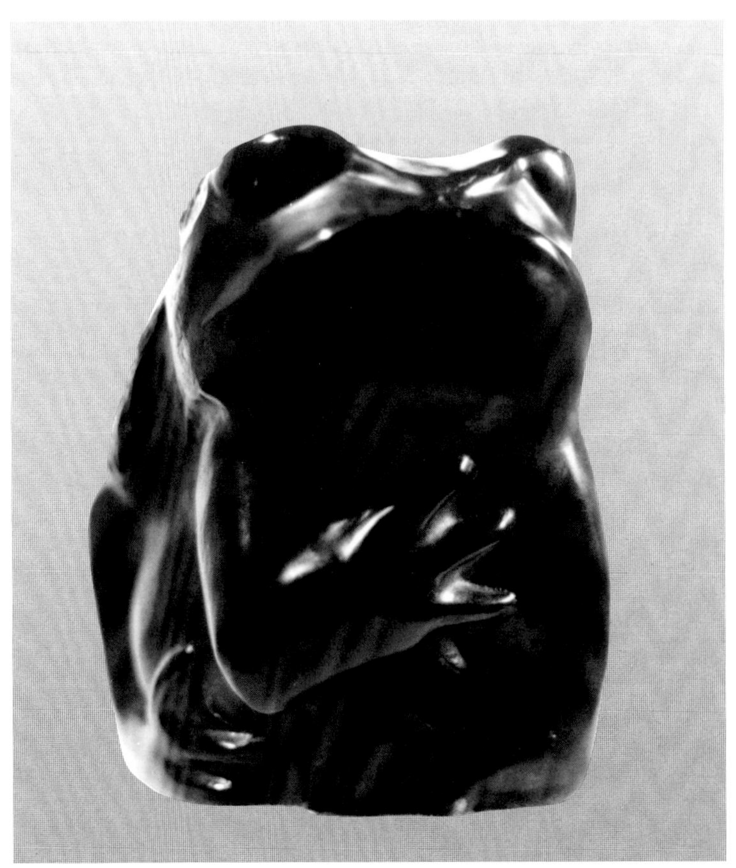

4 Amorous Toad, *bronze*

5 Amorous Toad, *bronze*

6 Chouette, *bronze*

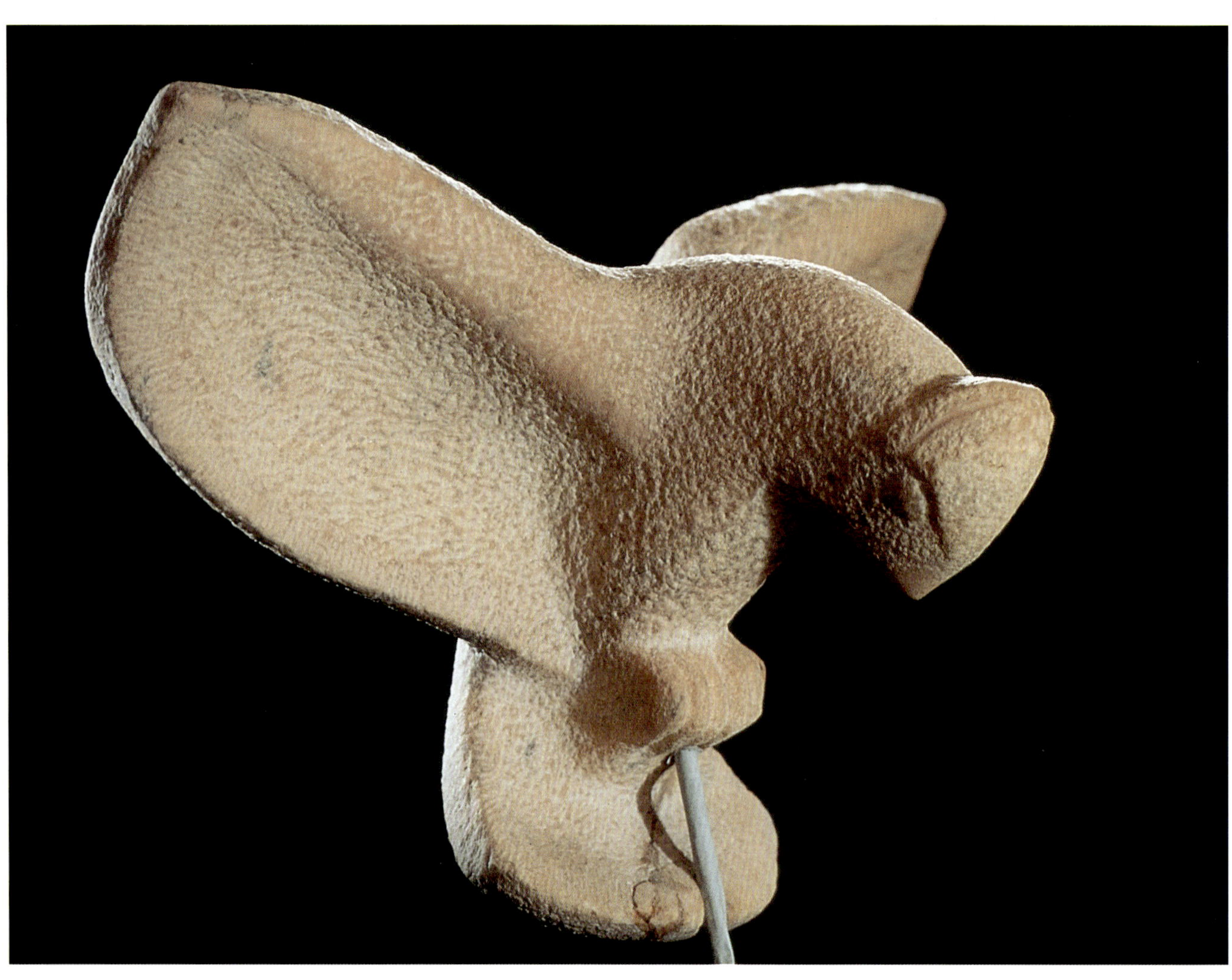

7 Cardinal in Flight, *pink marble*

8 Ancient Horse, *bronze*
9 Hare, *bronze*

10 Pigeon, *bronze*

11 Bird, *alabaster*

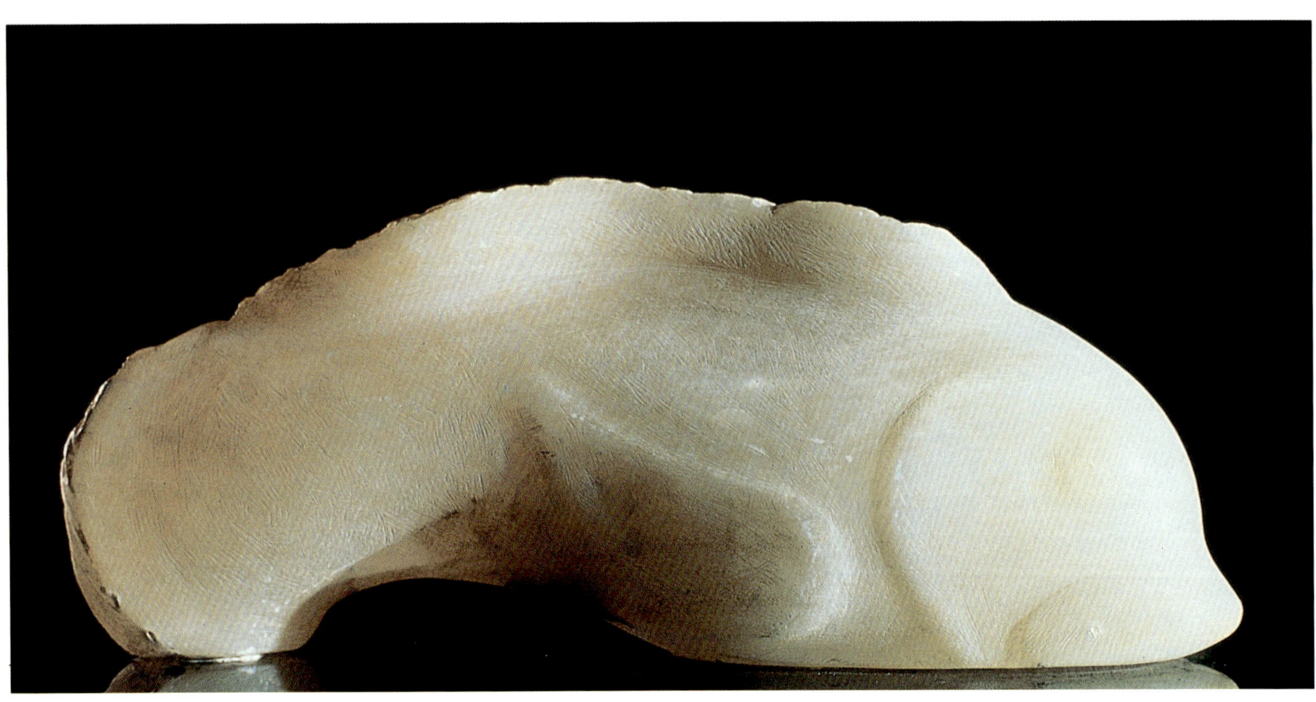

12 Fish III, *alabaster*

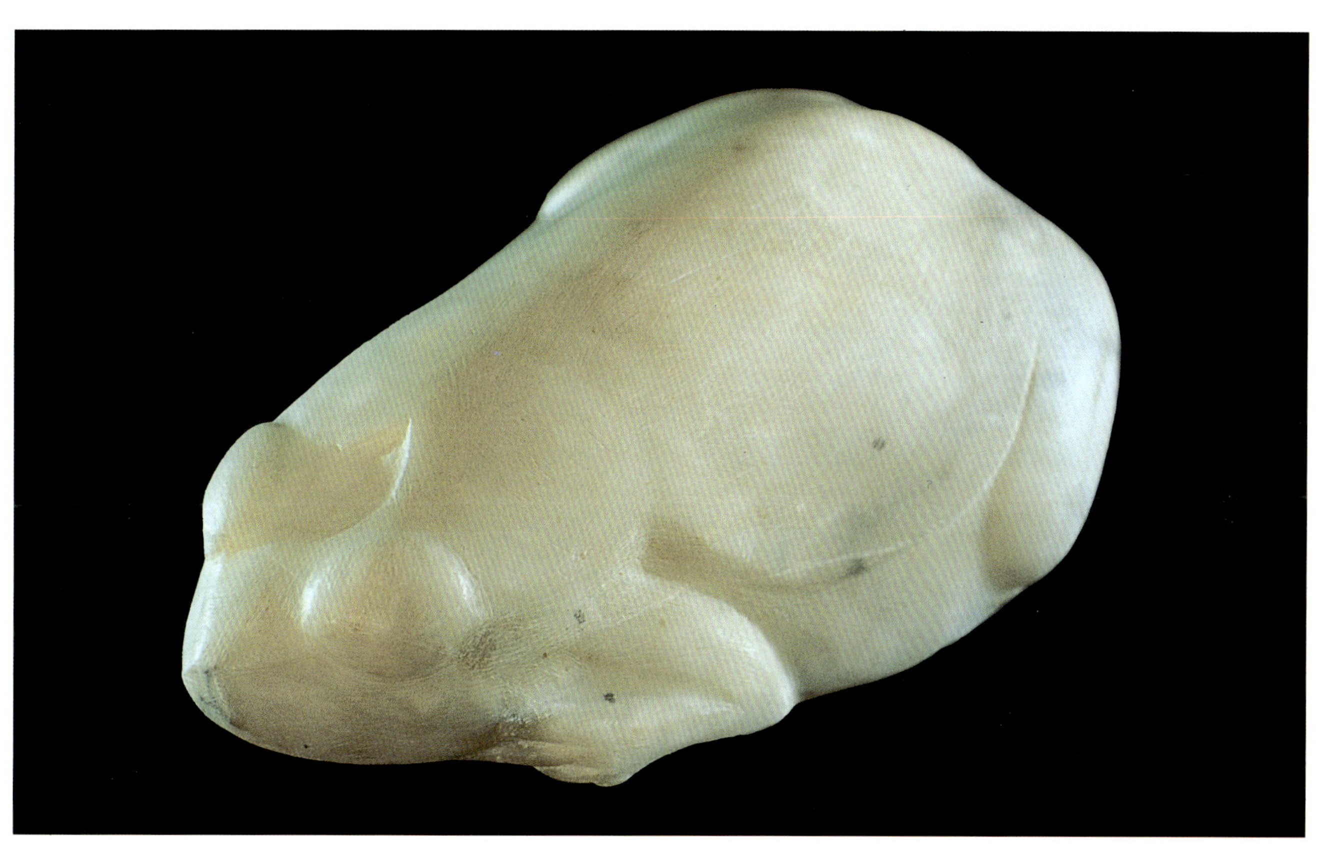

13 SLEEPING FROG, *alabaster*

14 ÉPERVIER, *bronze*

15 Épervier, *bronze*

16 Barn Owl, *bronze*

17 Barn Owl, *alabaster*

18 Nada, *marble*

19 Firebird, *bronze*

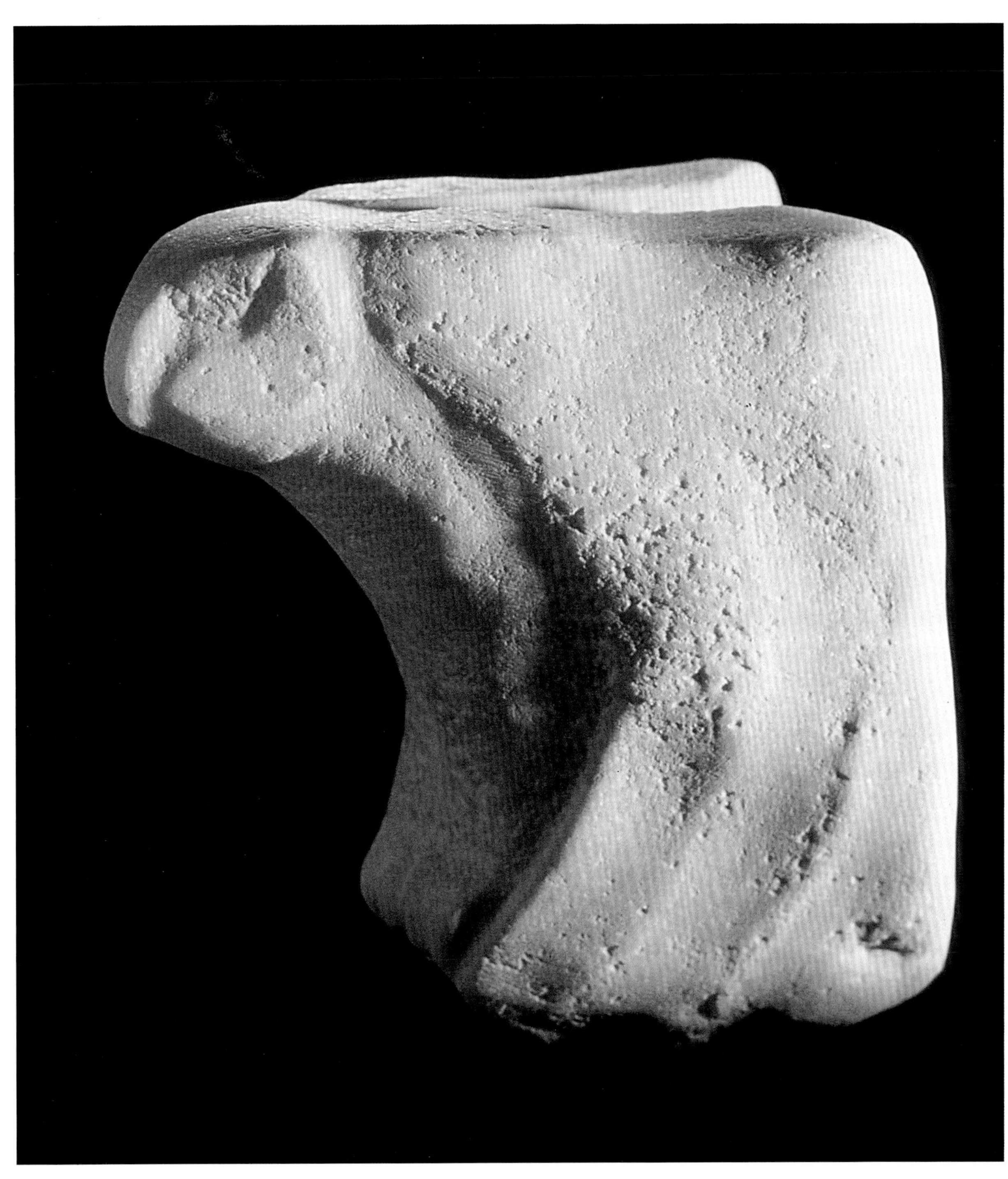

20 Delphi Eagle, *Greek marble*

21 La Belle Italienne, *bronze*

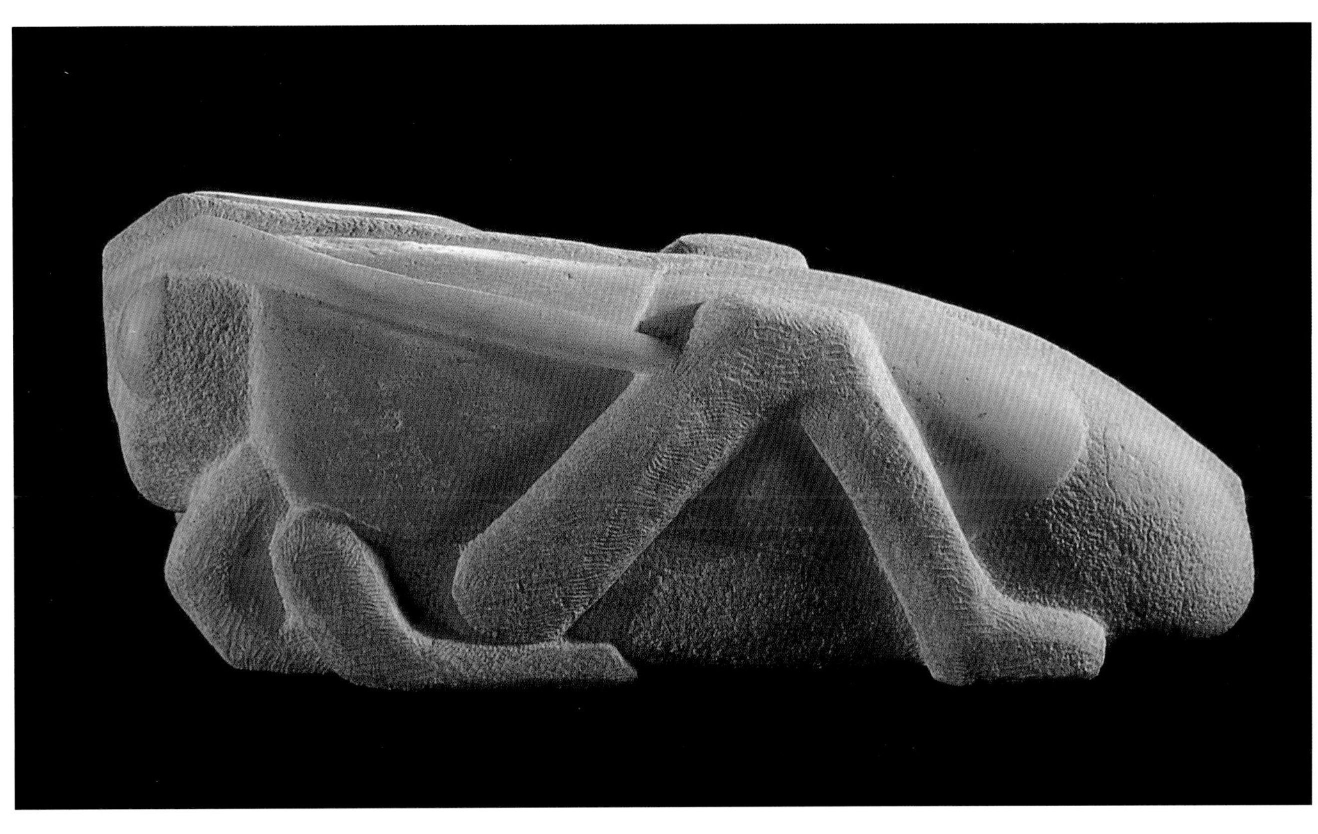

22 Locust, *onyx*

23 JUMPING FISH, *bronze*

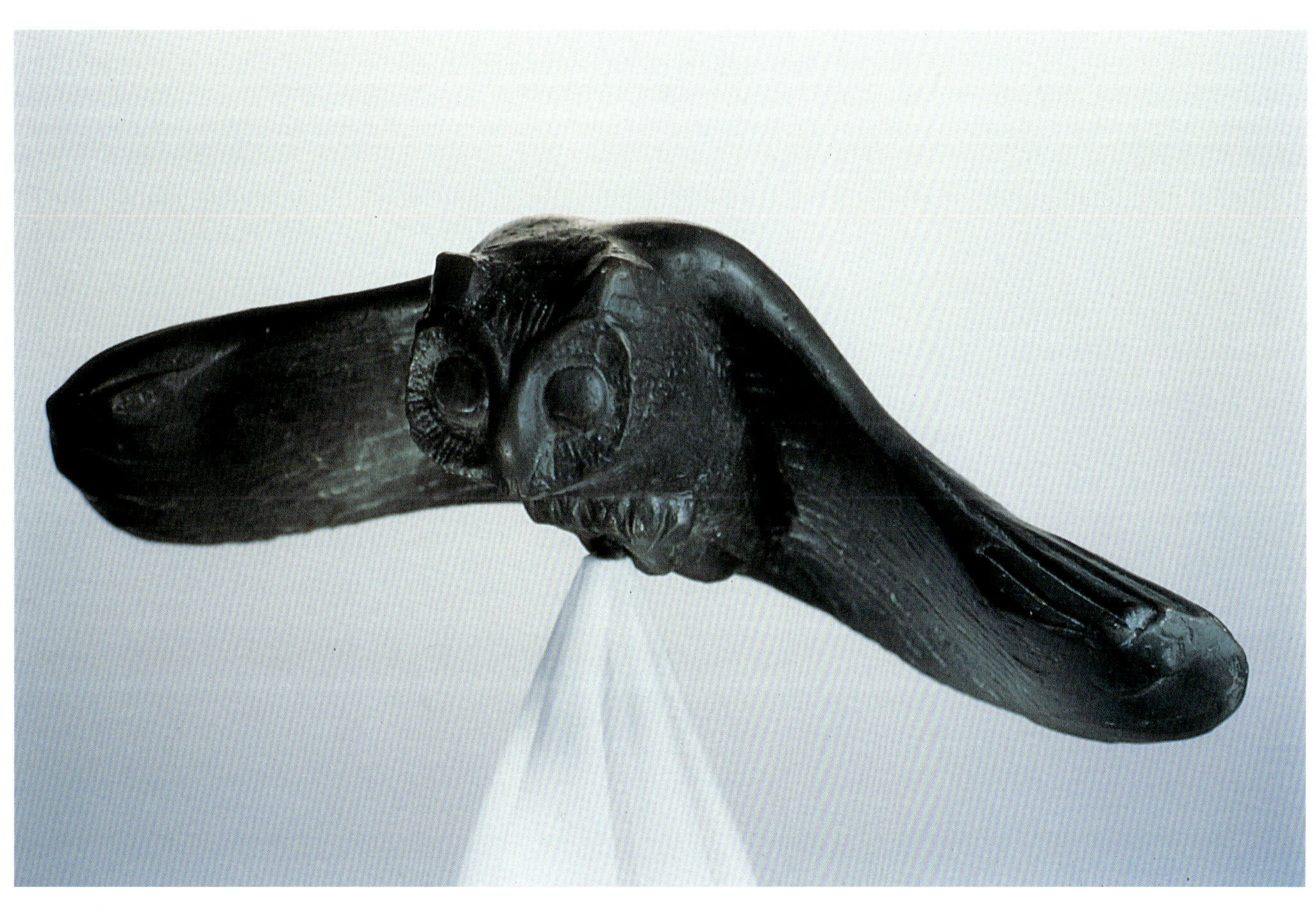

24 Owl in Flight, *bronze*

25 Butterfly, *onyx*

26 SMALL SWAN, *bronze*

27 Blue Eagle, *marble*

28 Large Bull, *marble*

29 Heraldic Eagle, *bronze*

30 Heraldic Eagle, *marble*

1965–1978

31 Praying Mantis, *onyx*

32 Colt, Head Turned, *marble*

33 COLT, HEAD TURNED, *golden bronze*
34 COLT, HEAD TURNED, *bronze*

35 Hawk, *bronze*

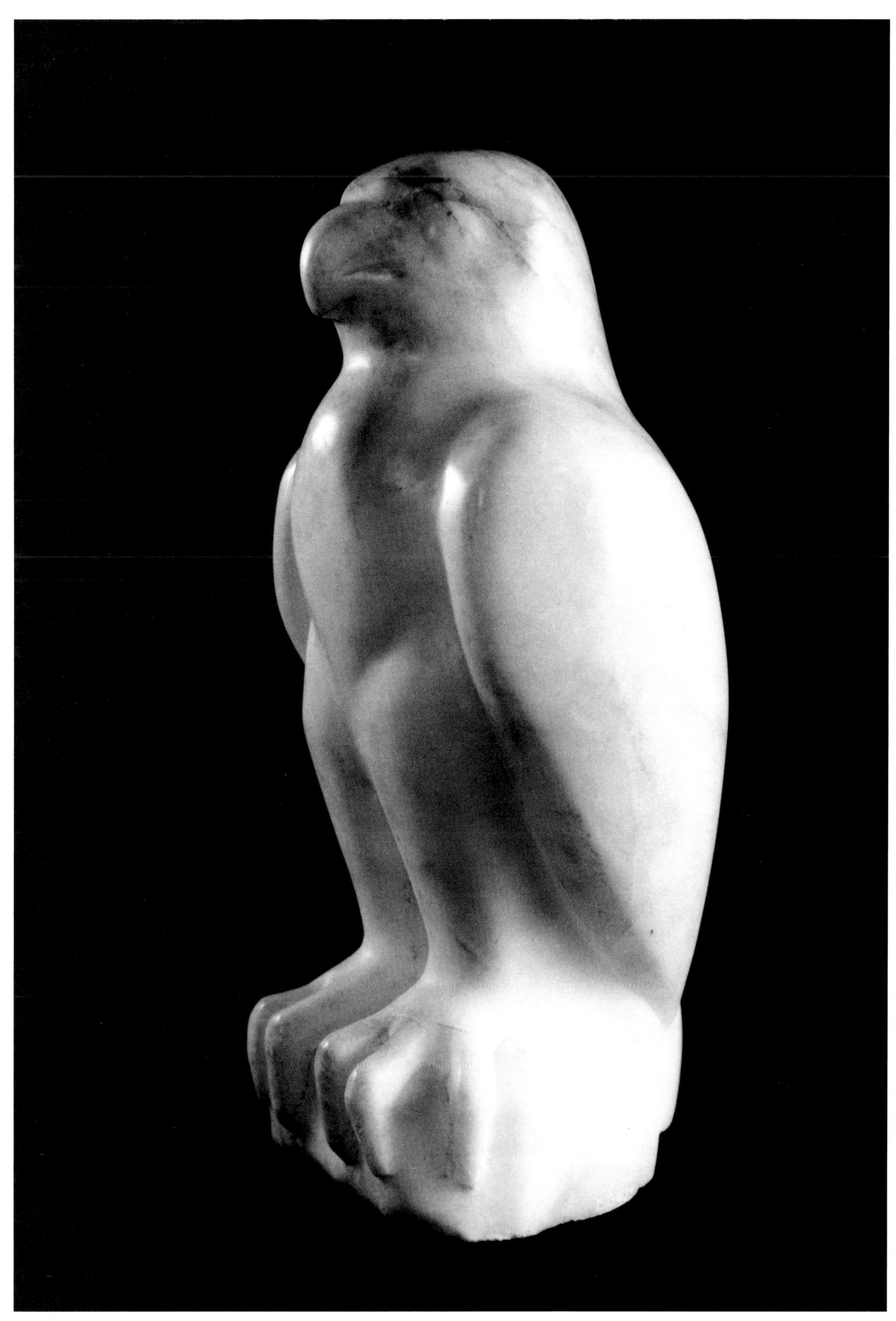

36 Hawk, *alabaster*

37 Melanie (Desert Fox), *bronze*

38 FENNEC, *bronze*

39 La Nuit (detail), *marble*

40 La Nuit, *marble*

41 Mother and Son (detail), *granite*

42 Mother and Son, *granite*

43 Fallen Horse (study), *marble*

44 Cobra, *bronze*

45 Giant Snail, *alabaster*

46 Snail, *alabaster*

47 Cobra, *alabaster*

48 Large Hawk, *bronze*

49 Hill Ponies, *alabaster*

50 Raven, *black granite*

51 Large Swan, *alabaster*

52 Moon Dragons, *alabaster*

53 Sea Hawk, *onyx*

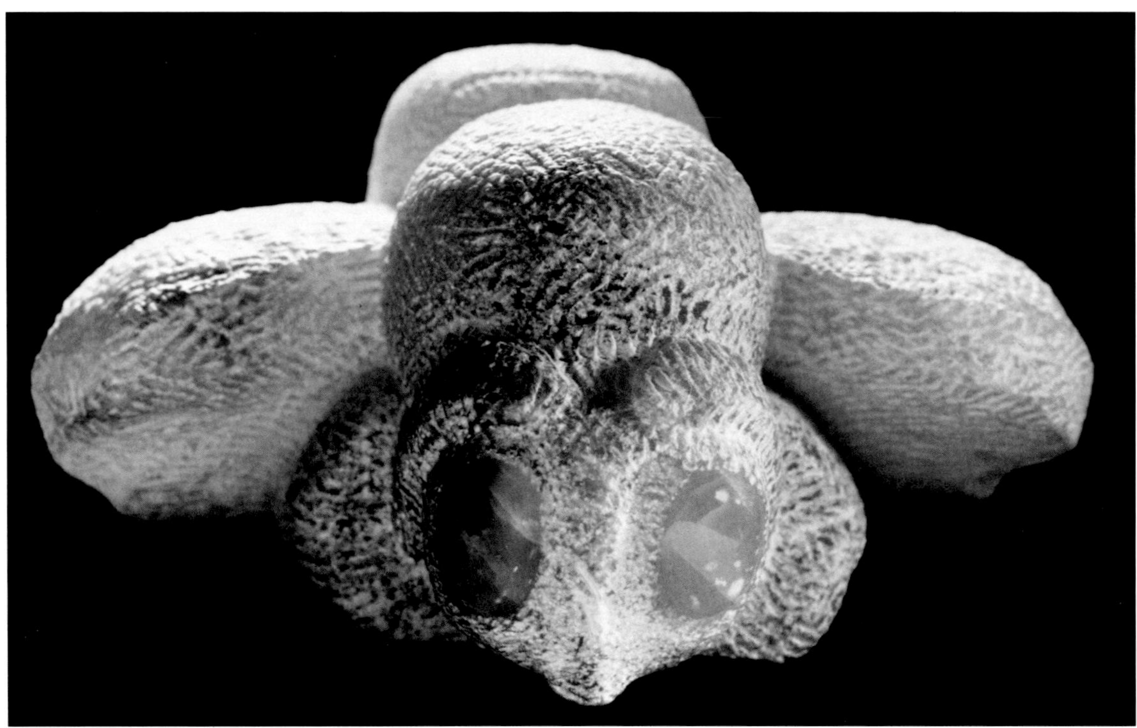

54 TIBETAN PONY, *bronze*

55 BEE, *alabaster*

56 Tibetan Pony, *alabaster*

57 Europa (detail), *granite*
58 Europa, *bronze*

59 Europa (detail), *granite*

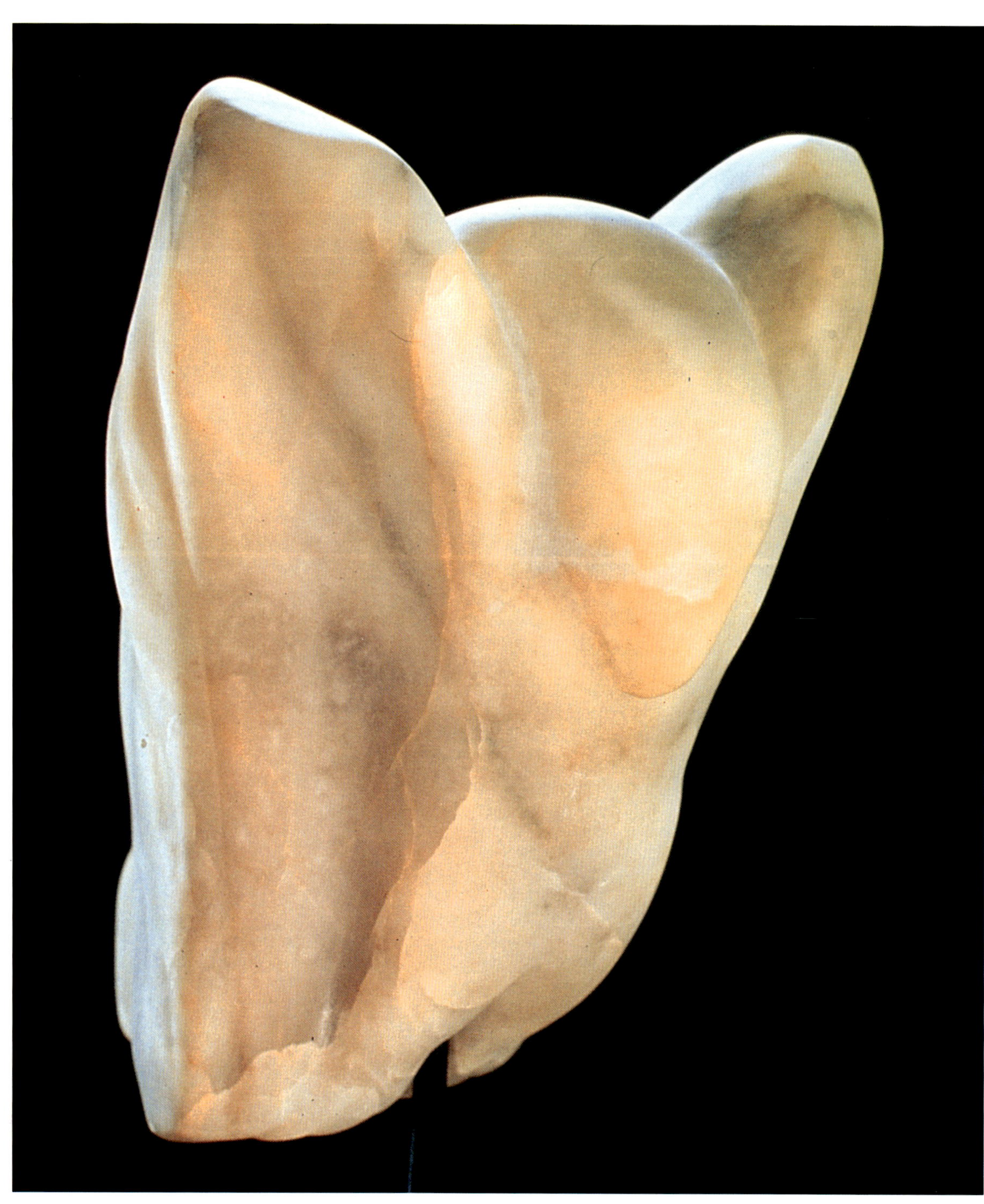

60 Eagle, *alabaster*

61 Eagle, *bronze*

62 Fallen Horse, *Volterra marble*

1978–1992

63 Open Magnolia, *alabaster*

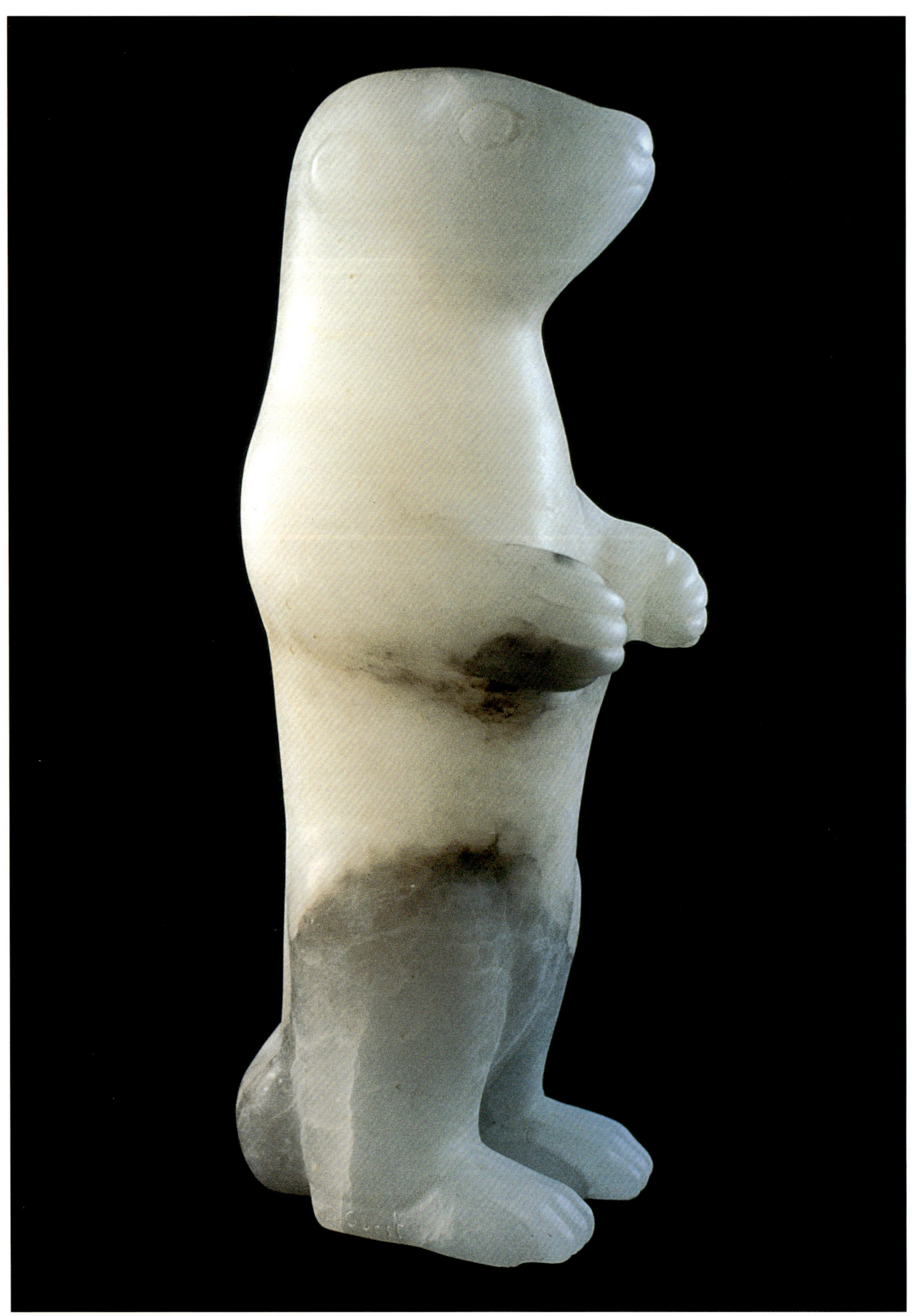

64 Marmotte, *alabaster*

65 Marmotte, *bronze*

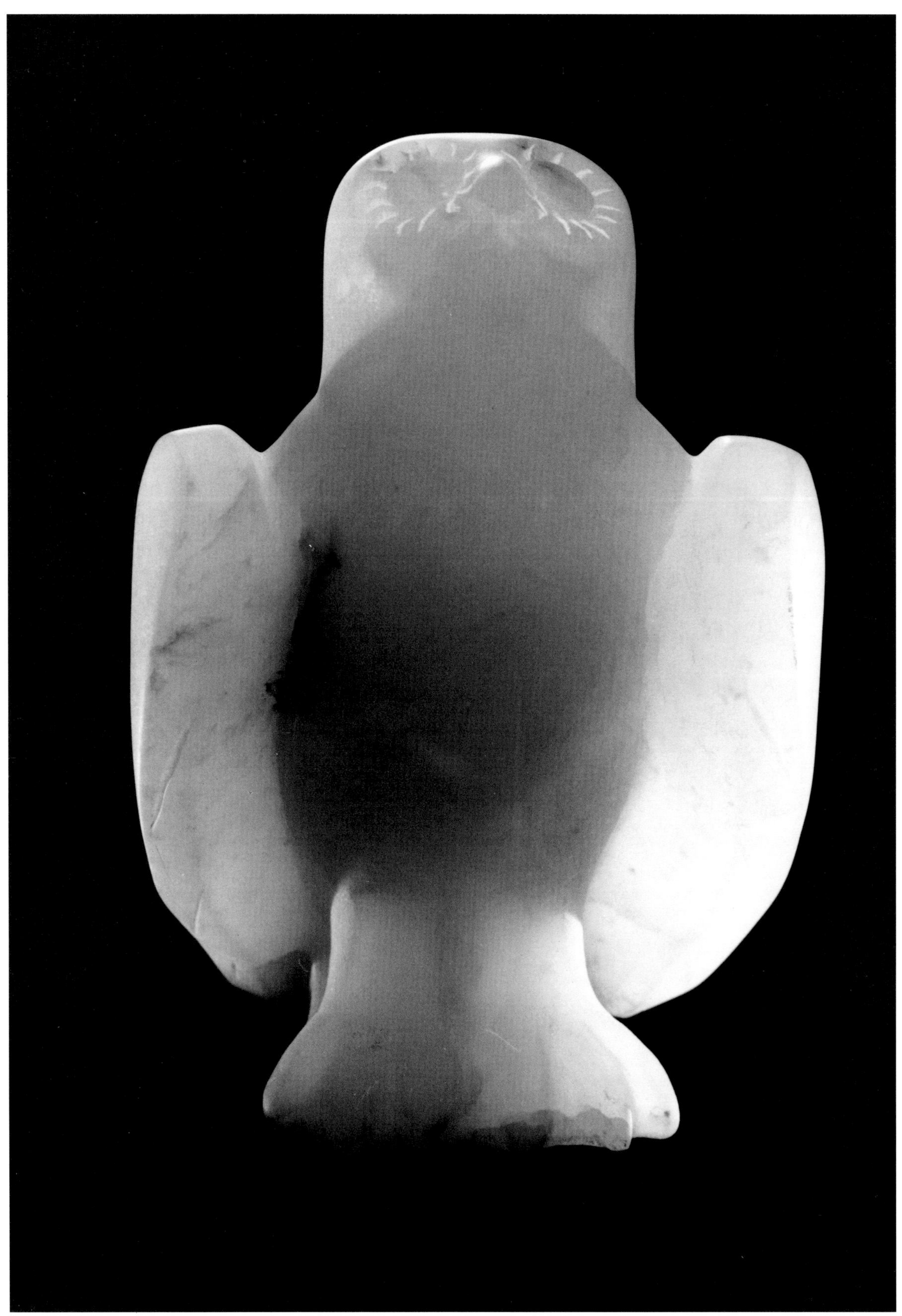

66 Owl Praying, *bronze*

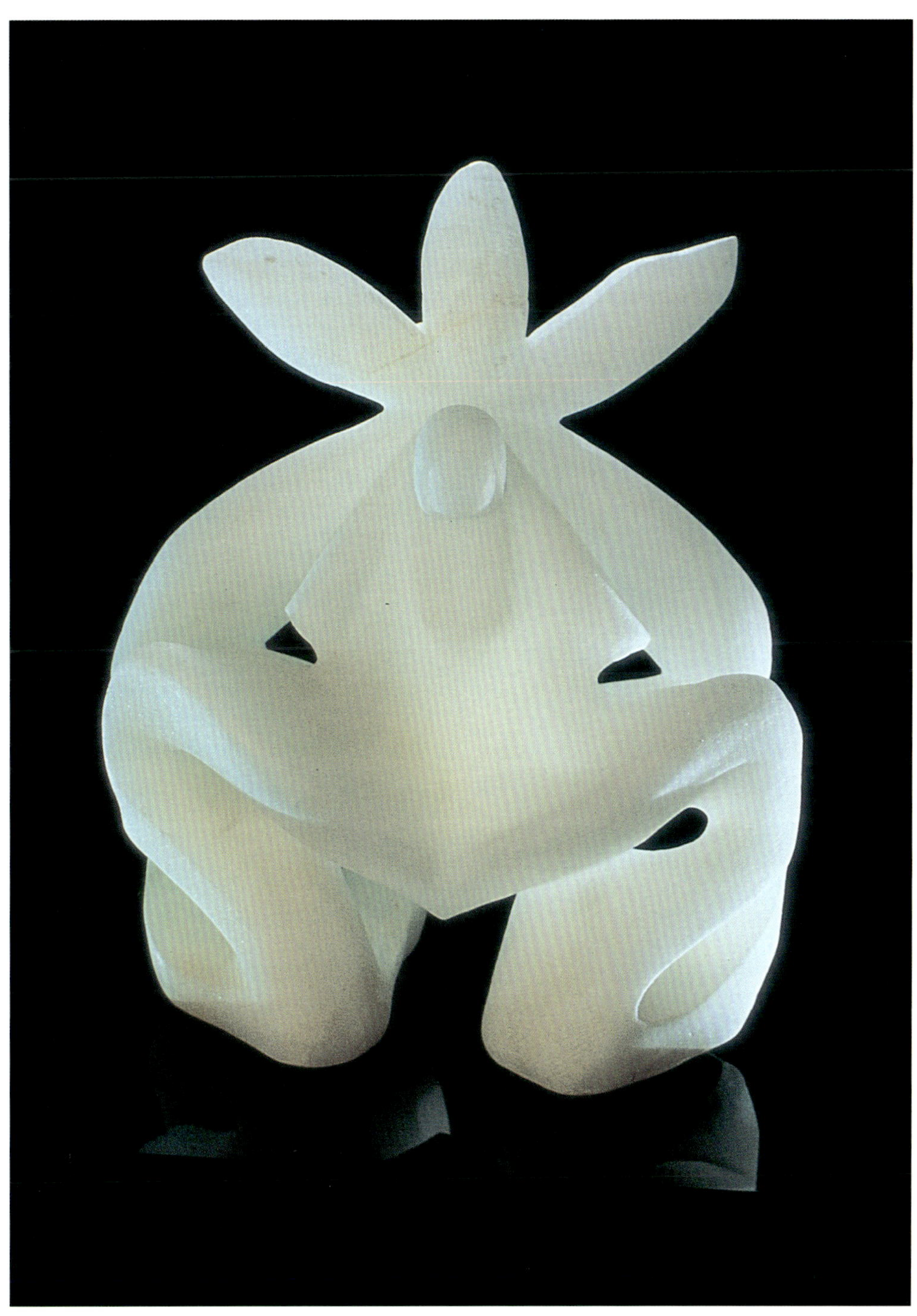

67 Ghost Orchid, *alabaster*

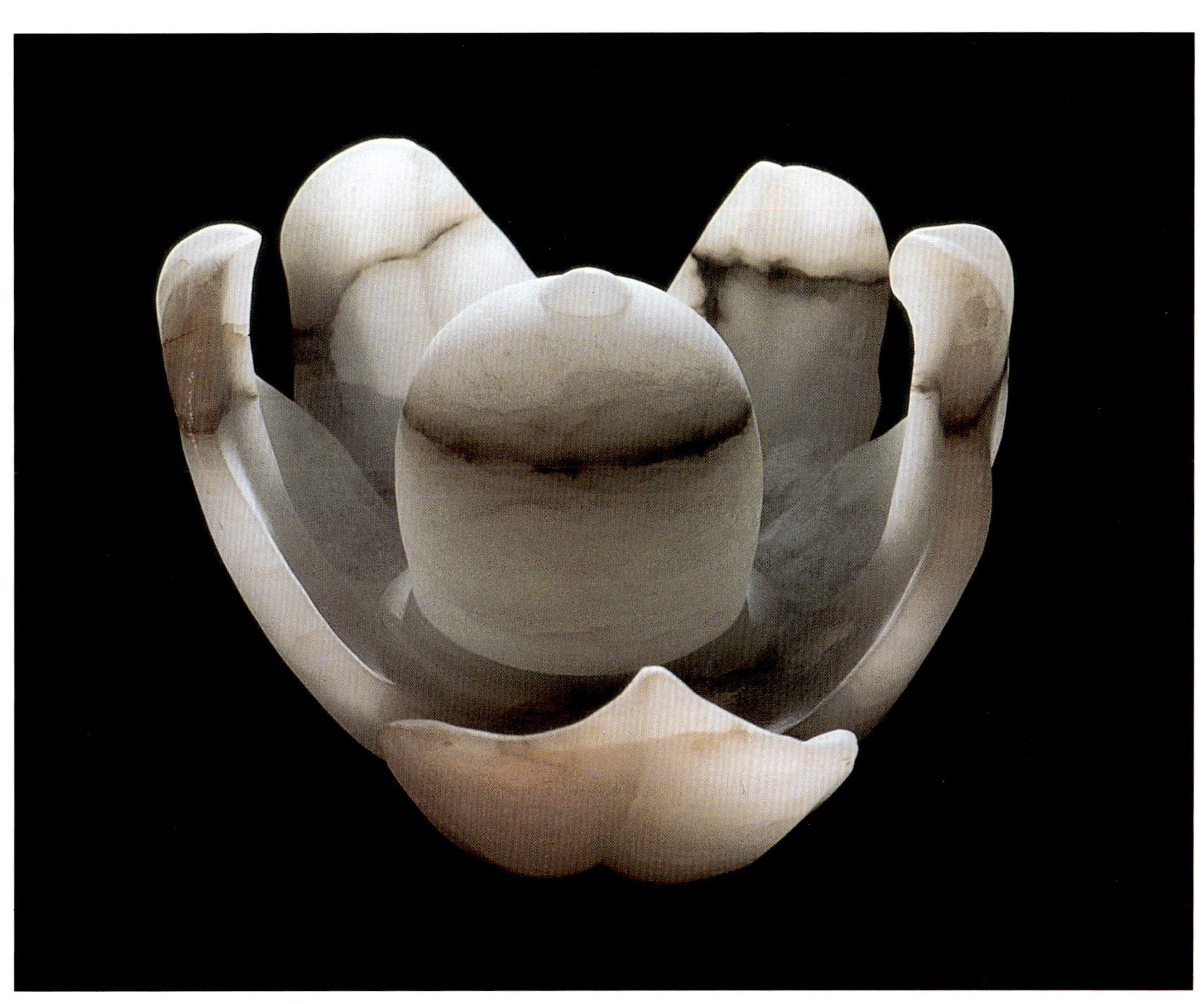

68 ACANTHE, *alabaster*

69 Small Magnolia, *alabaster*
70 Magnolia I, *alabaster*

71 Rose, *red alabaster*

72 Flamingo's Head, *bronze*

73 Woodcock, *bronze*

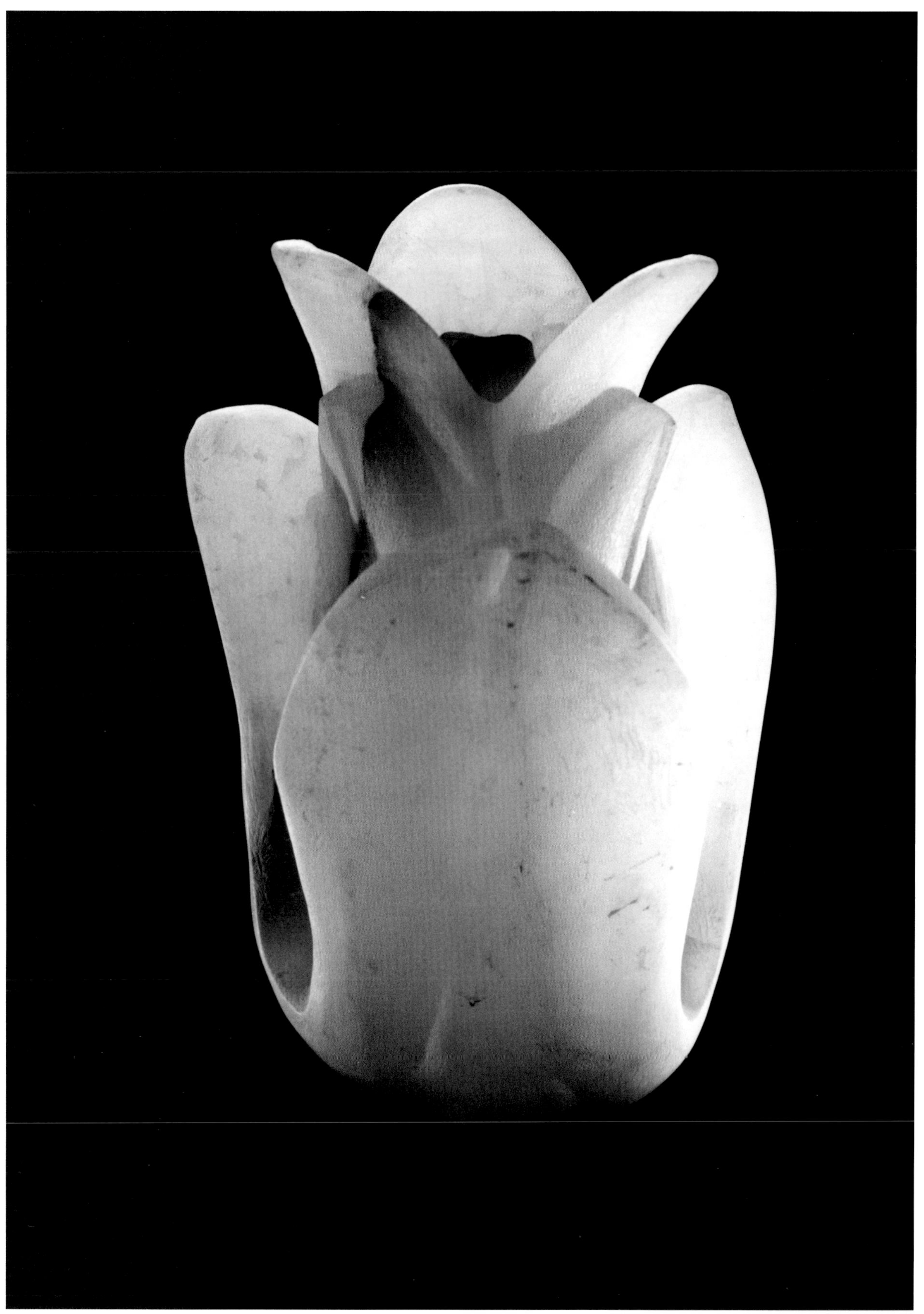

74 TULIP, *alabaster*

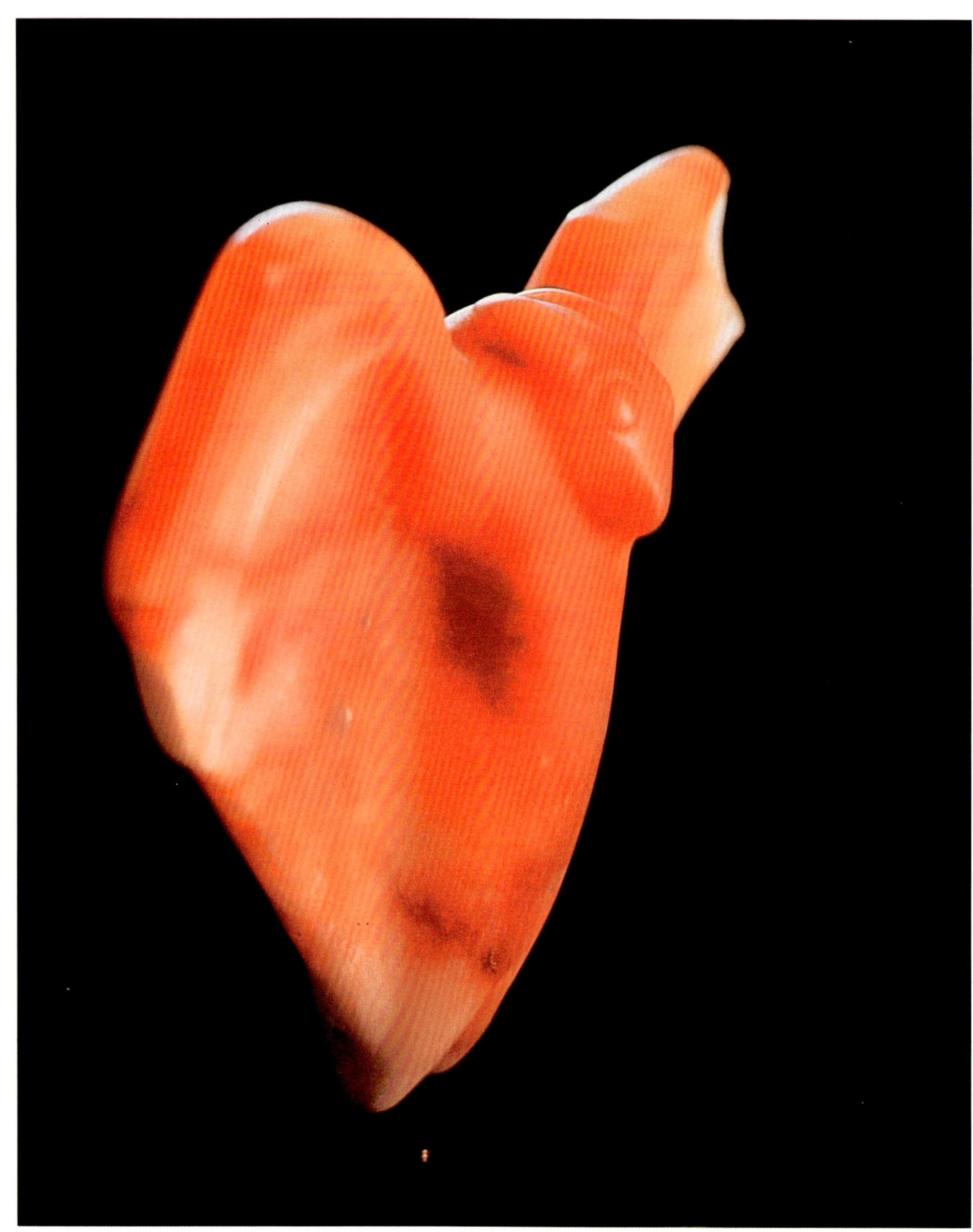

75 Bat, *red alabaster*

76 Fish IV, *alabaster*

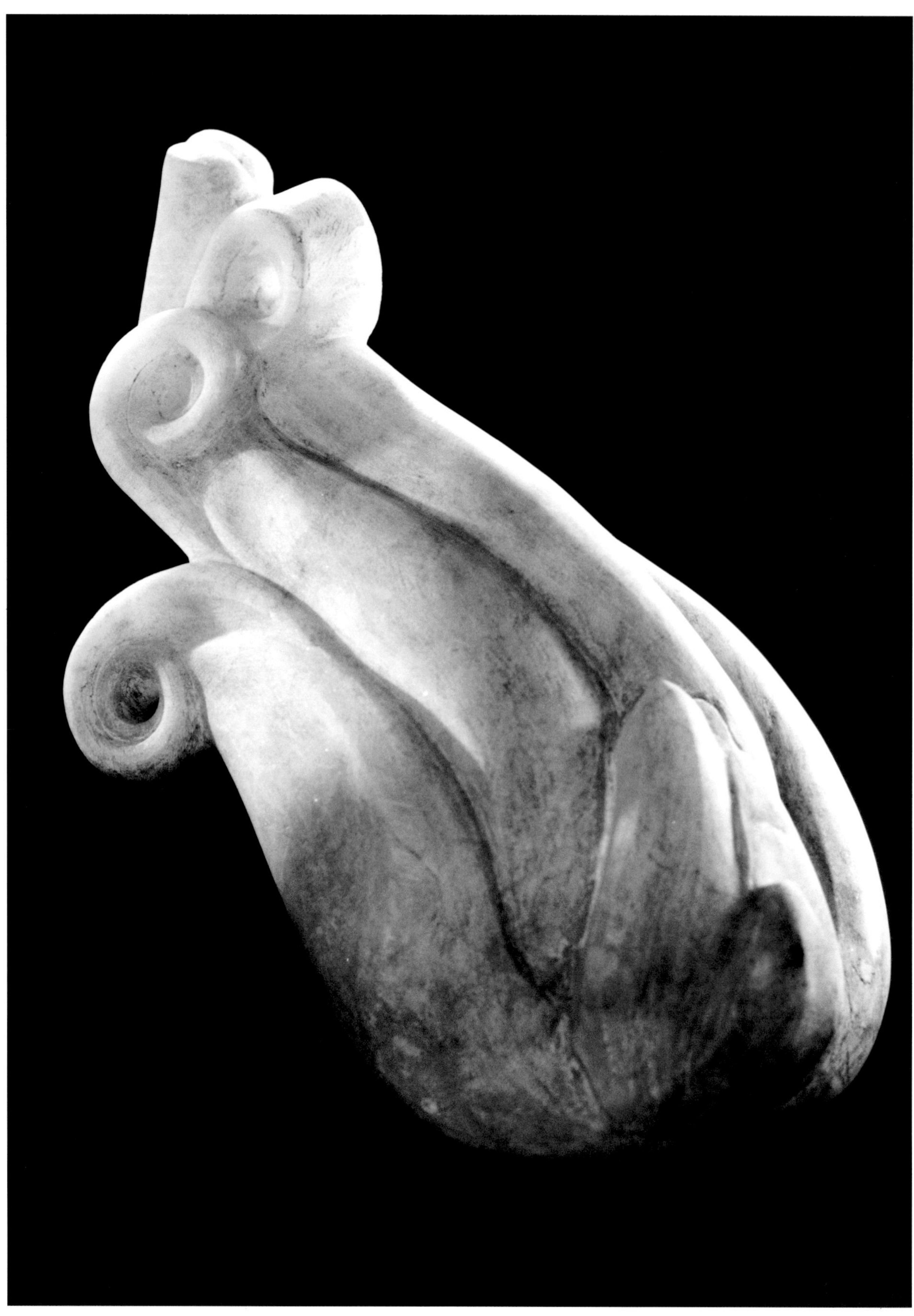

77 Tropical Flower, *alabaster*

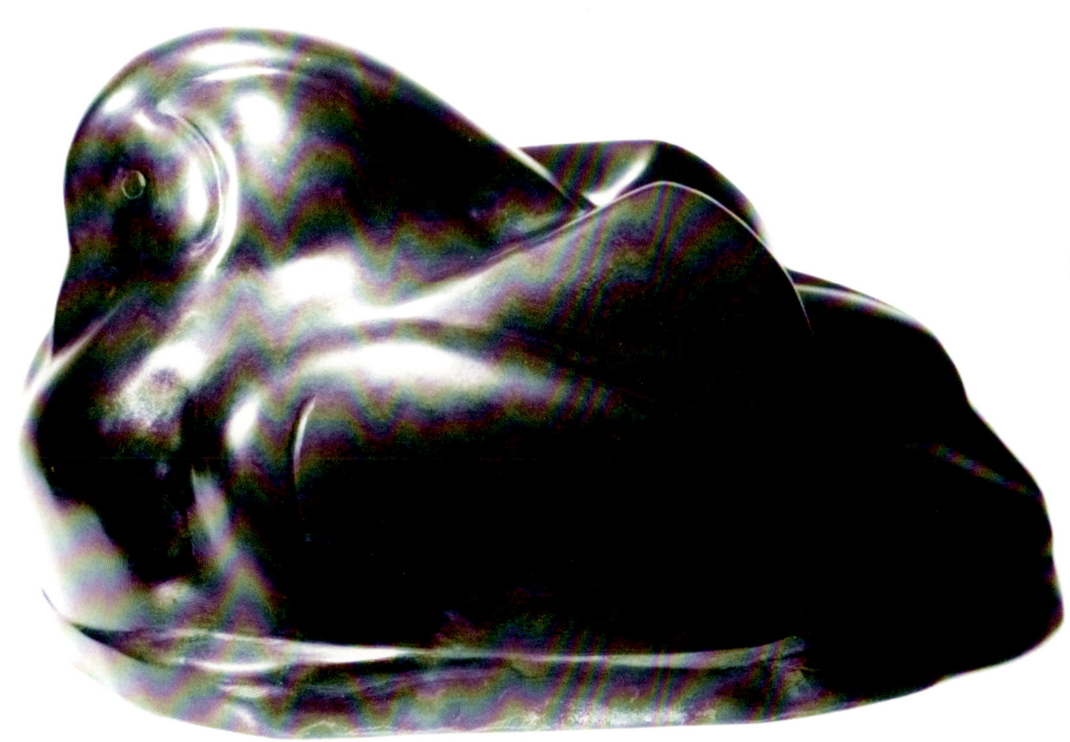

78 QUAIL, *golden bronze*
79 MANDARIN DUCK, *bronze*

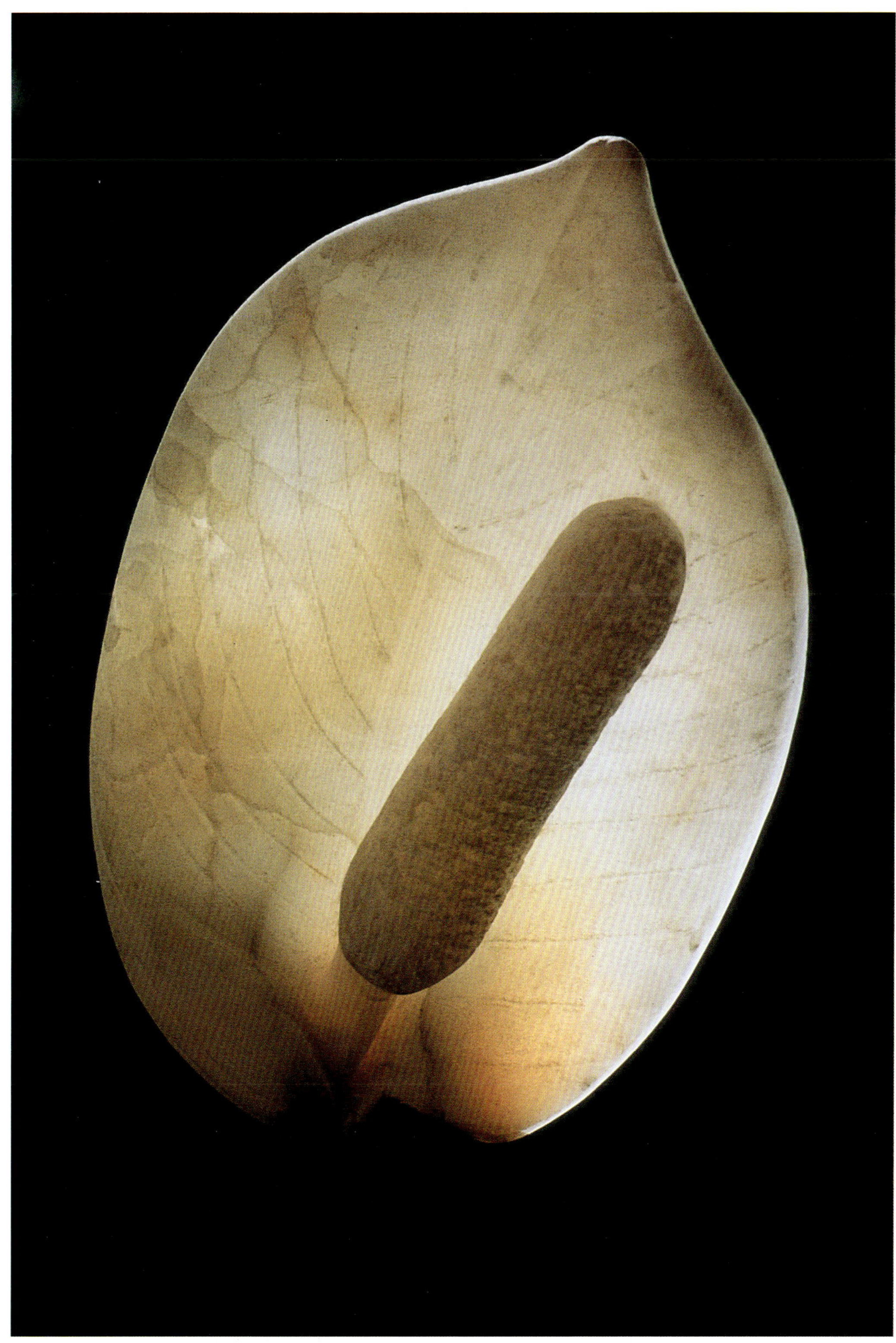

80 White Sail, *alabaster*

81 CHEETAH'S HEAD, *bronze*

82 Giant Toad, *bronze*

83 Mycenaean Bull's Head, *bronze*

84 Mountain Sheep, *dark bronze*

85 Ram's Head, *bronze*

86 Angry Owl, *bronze*

87 Tree Frog II, *bronze*

88 Sweet Pea, *alabaster*

89 Tree Frog II, *alabaster*

90 Tree Frog I, *soapstone*

91 Water Lily, *alabaster*

92 ANTHURIUM III, *alabaster*

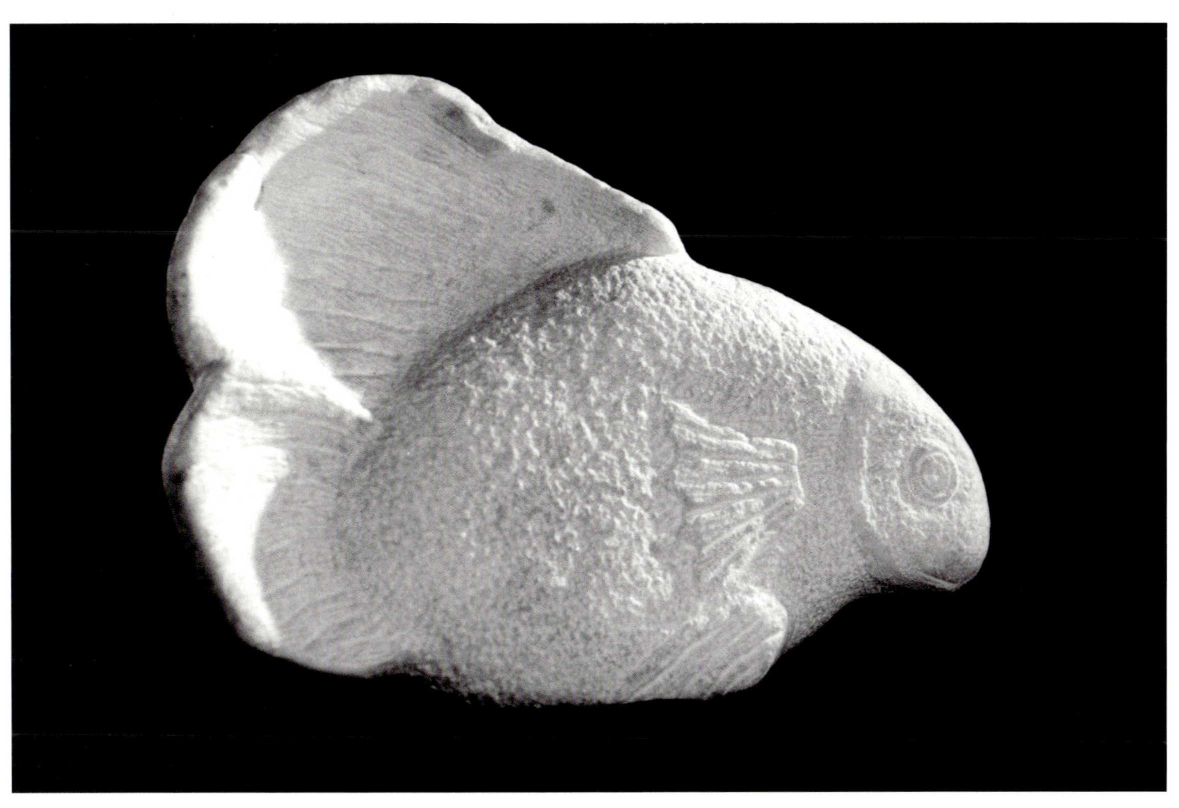

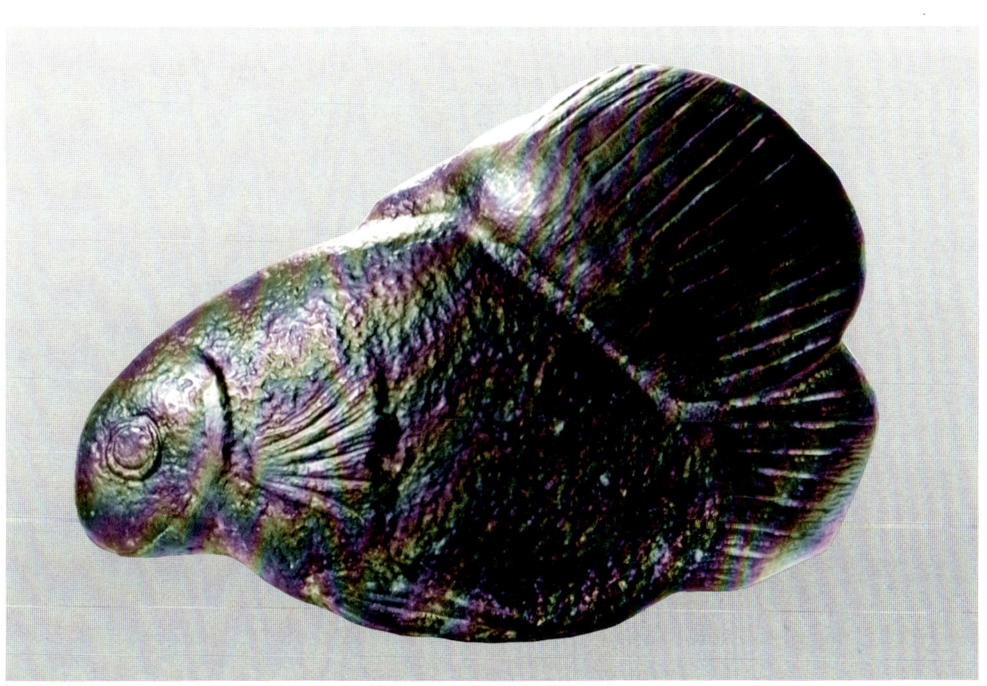

93 Fish I, *alabaster*
94 Fish I, *bronze*

95 Hovering Owl, *bronze*
96 Dove Flying, *alabaster*

97 Hovering Owl, *alabaster*

98 LOTUS I, *alabaster*

99 Lotus III, *alabaster*

100 Salamander, *alabaster*
101 Lotus Leaf, *marble*

102 SALAMANDER, *bronze*

103 Trillium, *alabaster*

104 Swallow, *alabaster*

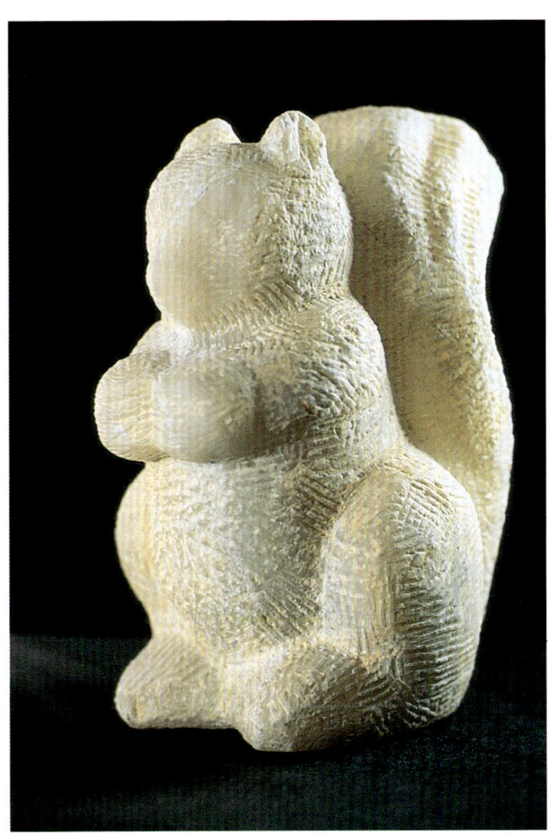

105 Swallow, *bronze*
106 Squirrel, *alabaster*

107 SUNFLOWER, *alabaster*
108 RHODODENDRON, *alabaster*

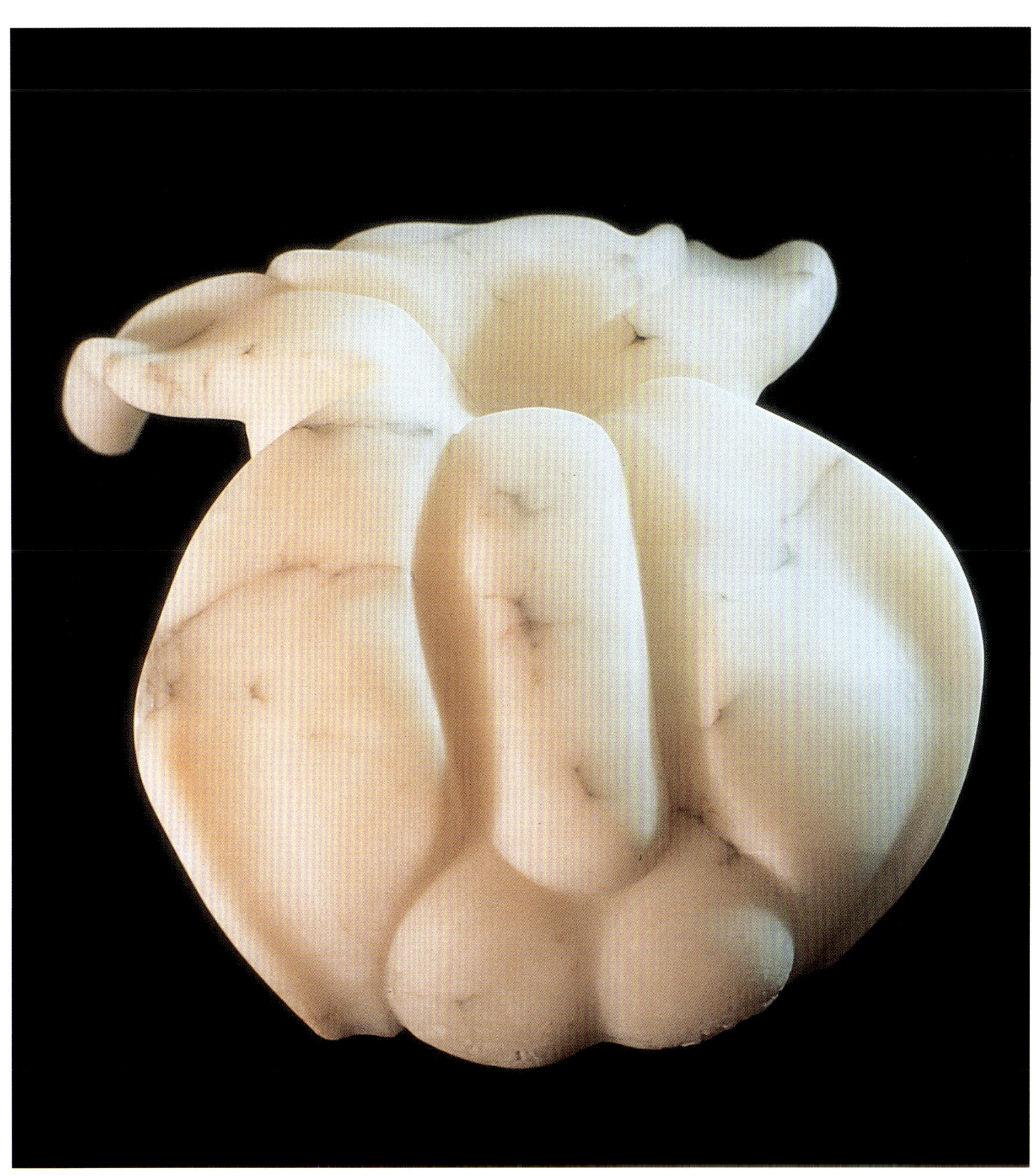

109 Orchid, *alabaster*

110 Monarch Butterfly, *alabaster*

111 Iris, *alabaster*

112 Hibiscus, *alabaster*

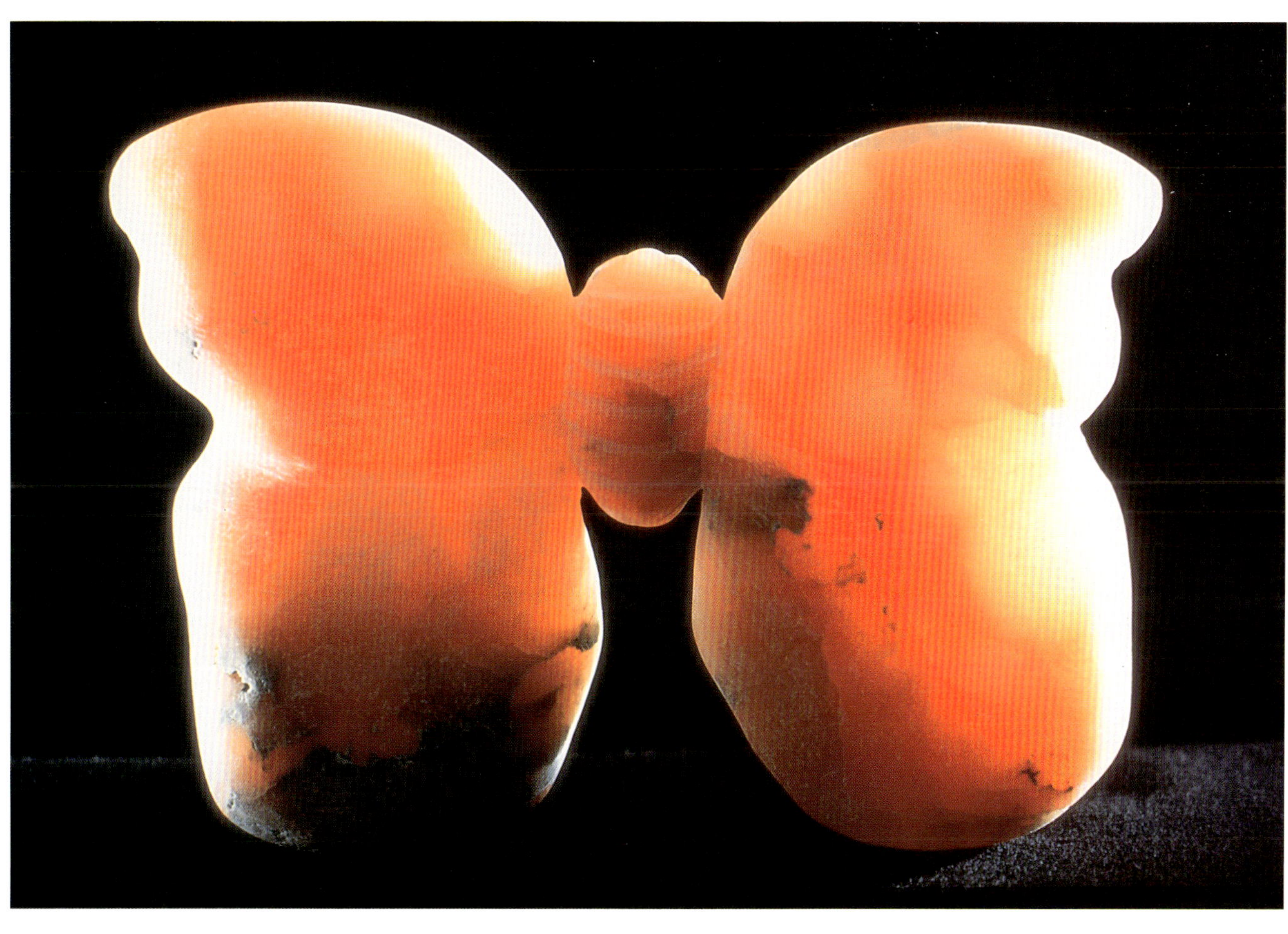

113 Butterfly, *red alabaster*

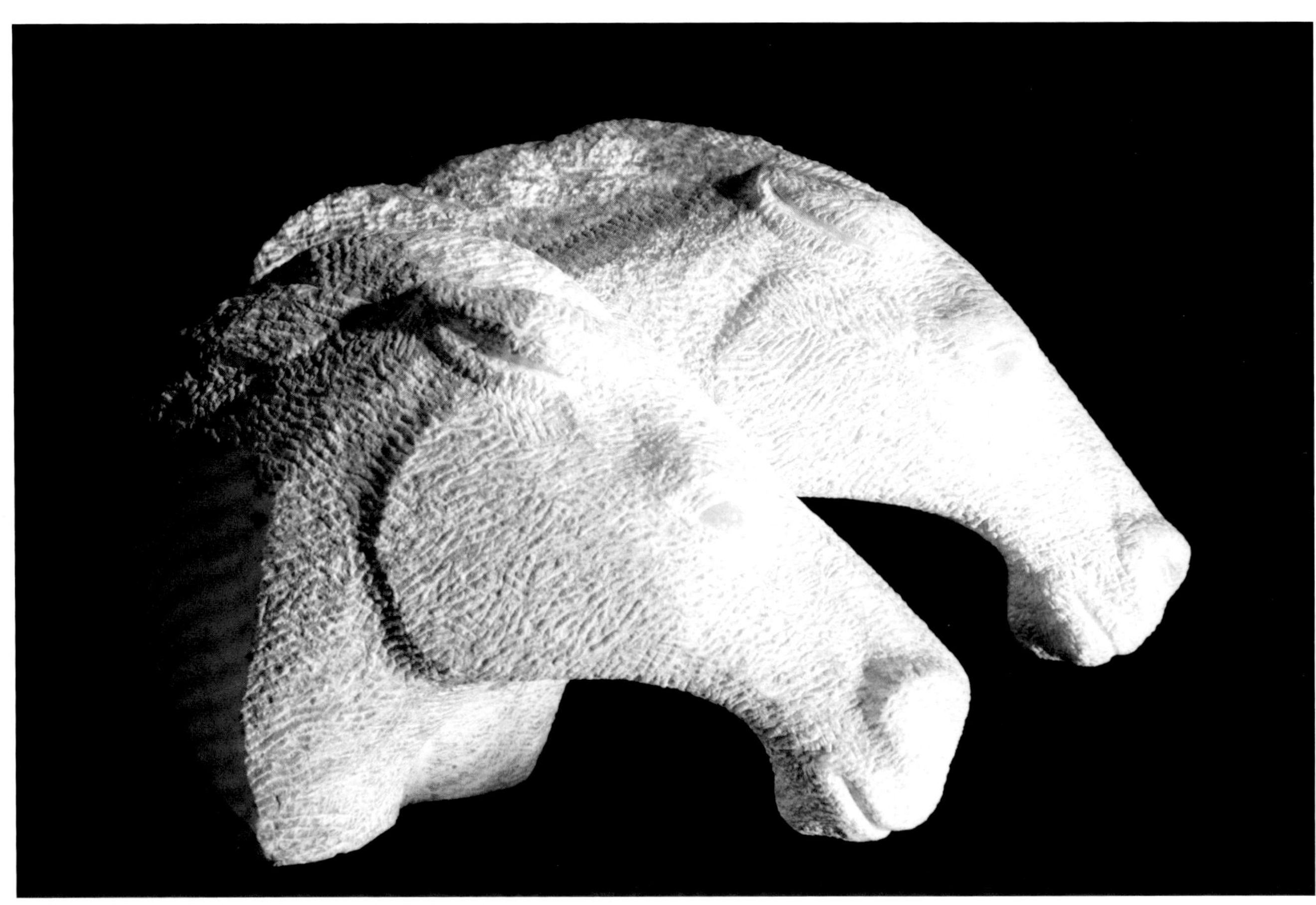

114 PHOTO FINISH, *alabaster*

115 Photo Finish, *original alabaster and bronze cast*

116 JACK IN THE PULPIT, *alabaster*

117 Closed Tulip, *alabaster*

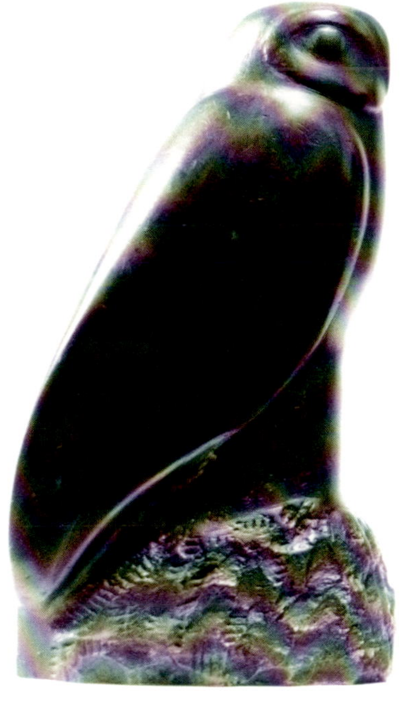

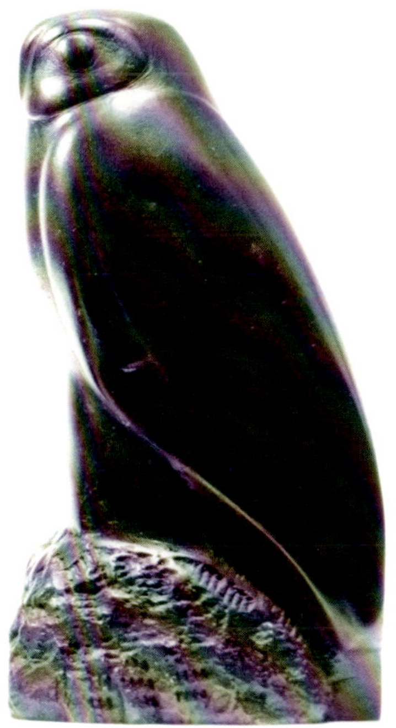

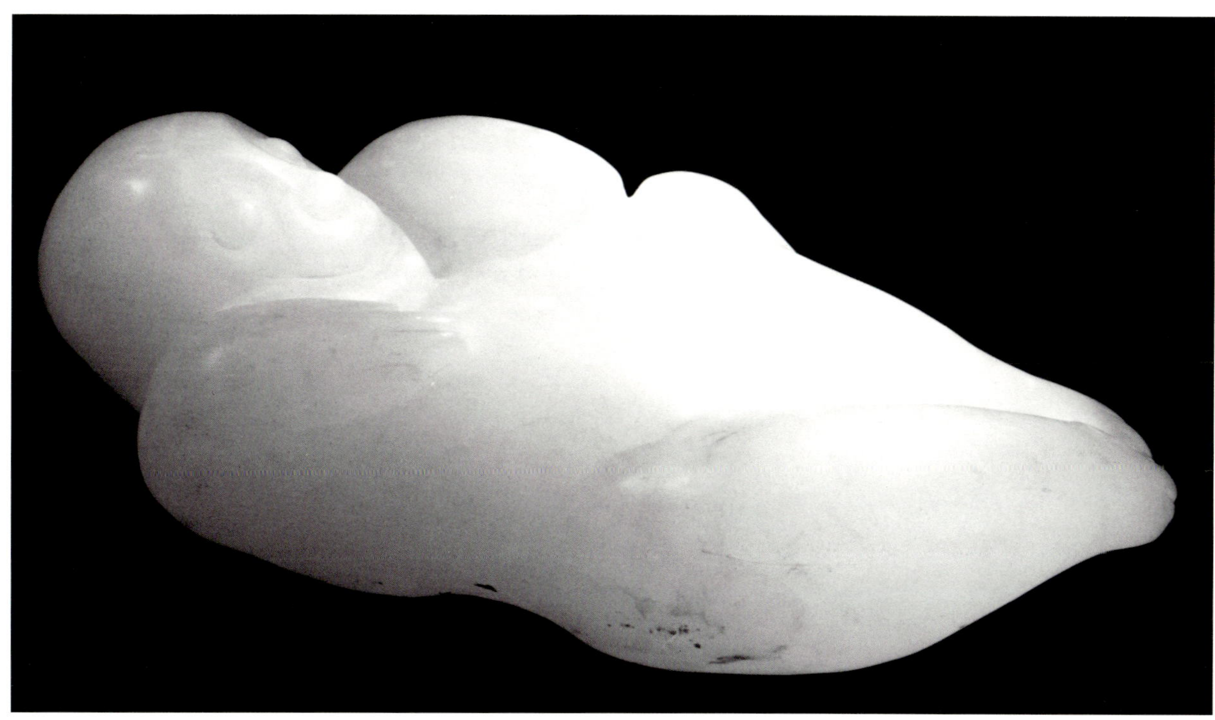

118 Sparrow Hawk, *soapstone*

119 Baby Seal, *alabaster*

120 Poppy, *alabaster*

121 Bali Bird, *bronze*

122 Snowbird, *alabaster*

123 Red Rose, *red alabaster*

124 Moth, *pink alabaster*

125 Snake, *soapstone*

126 THE WAVE, *alabaster*

127 ANTHURIUM I, *alabaster*

128 DRANUNCULAS VULGARIS, *pink alabaster*

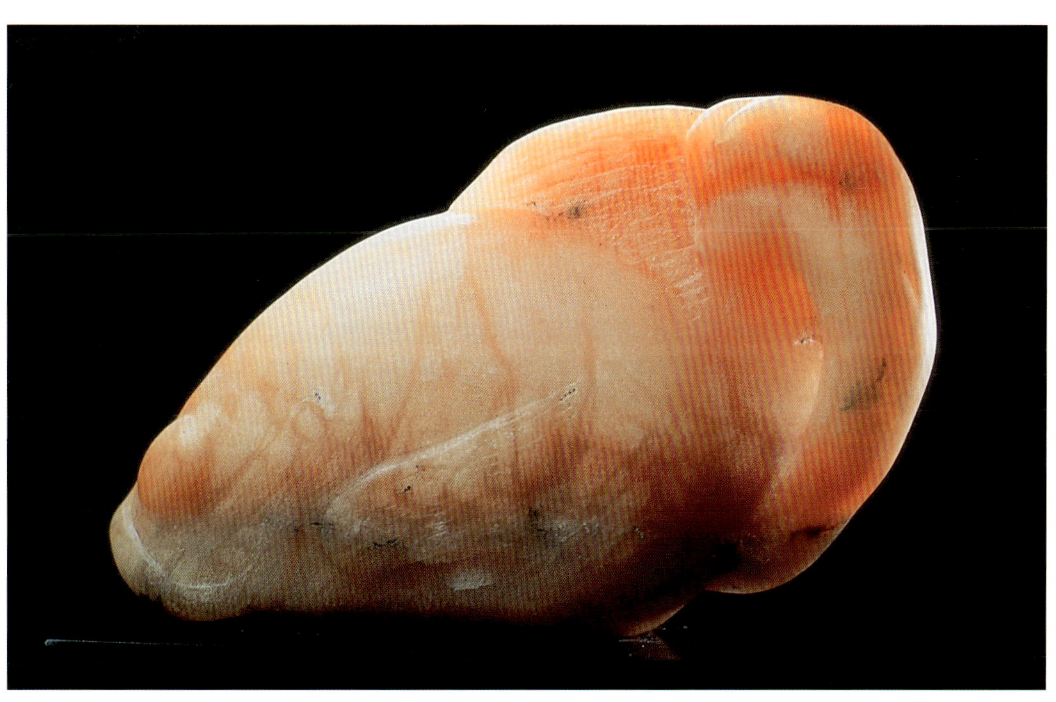

129 Oriental Goldfish, *alabaster*
130 Fish III, *bronze*

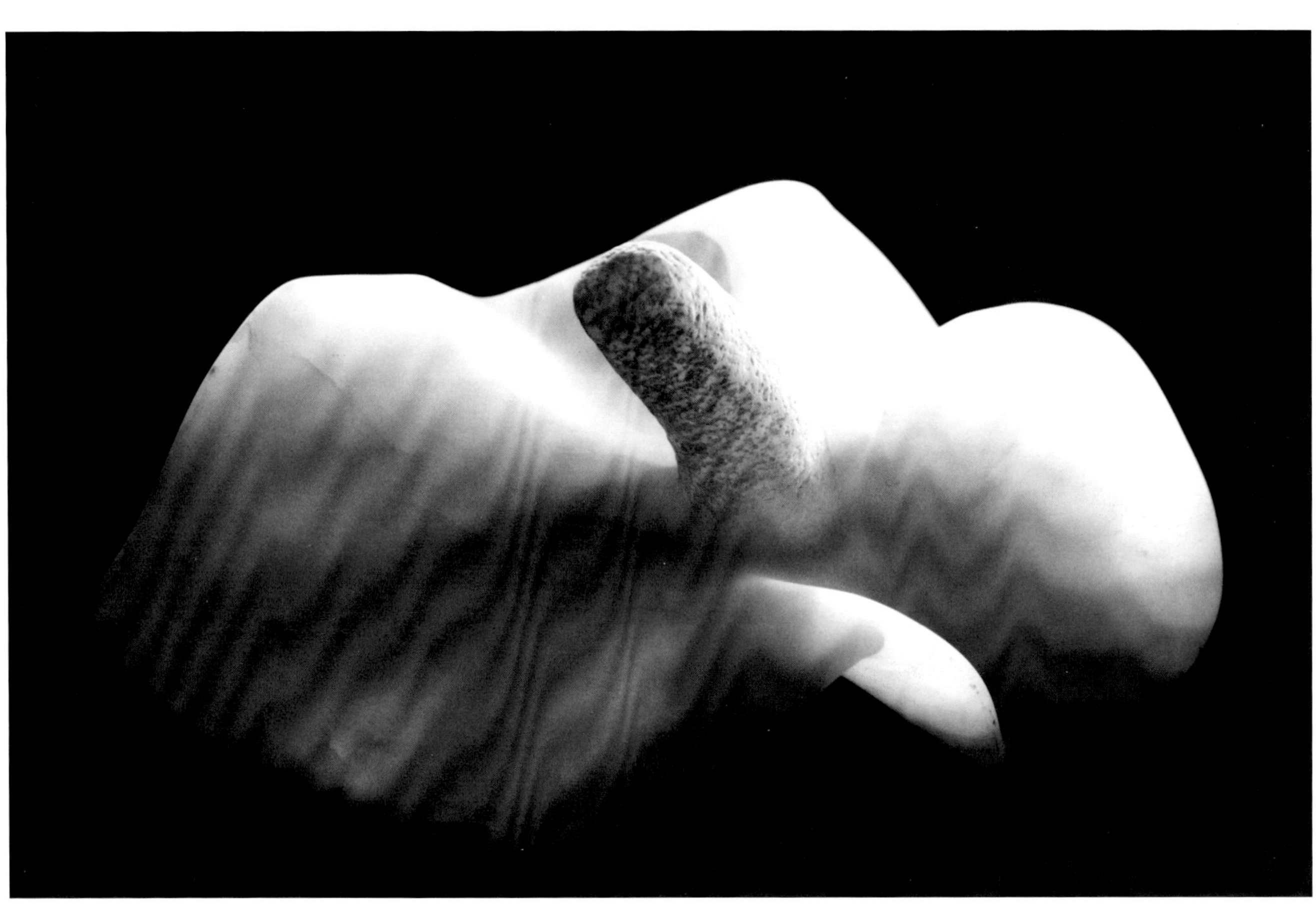

131 Anthurium II, *alabaster*

132 Mare and Foal, *alabaster*

133 Mare and Foal, *alabaster*

LIST OF PLATES

1 Grand Duc, *granite, 23½″ × 23″ × 59″*

2 Amorous Toad, *onyx, 11½″ × 7″ × 9½″*

3 Grand Duc, *granite, 23½″ × 23″ × 59″*

4 Amorous Toad, *bronze, 11½″ × 7″ × 9½″*

5 Amorous Toad, *bronze, 11½″ × 7″ × 9½″*

6 Chouette, *bronze, 5½″ × 6½″ × 11″*

7 Cardinal in Flight, *pink marble, 11½″ × 22″ × 15″*

8 Ancient Horse, *bronze, 17½″ × 6″ × 6½″*

9 Hare, *bronze, 17″ × 9½″ × 10½″*

10 Pigeon, *bronze, 10″ × 4″ × 7″*

11 Bird, *alabaster, 10″ × 4″ × 6″*

12 Fish III, *alabaster, 9″ × 4¼″ × 6¼″*

13 Sleeping Frog, *alabaster, 10¾″ × 8¼″ × 5″*

14 Épervier, *bronze, 18″ × 13″*

15 Épervier, *bronze, 18″ × 13″*

16 Barn Owl, *bronze, 25″ × 18″ × 24½″*

17 Barn Owl, *alabaster, 25″ × 18″ × 24½″*

18 Nada, *marble, 12½″ × 11⅔″ × 20″*

19 Firebird, *bronze, 16¾″ × 15½″ × 13¼″*

20 Delphi Eagle, *Greek marble, 19½″ × 11½″ × 14½″*

21 La Belle Italienne, *bronze, 15¾″ × 10½″ × 20″*

22 Locust, *onyx, 28½″ × 9″ × 10½″*

23 Jumping Fish, *bronze, 14½″ × 5½″ × 6″*

24 Owl in Flight, *bronze, 5″ × 19½″ × 8¼″*

25 Butterfly, *onyx, 18½″ × 6″ × 16″*

26 Small Swan, *bronze, 21″ × 10″ × 15″*

27 Large Bull, *marble (lost; approximately 48″ × 24″)*

28 Blue Eagle, *marble, 27″ × 10″*

29 Heraldic Eagle, *bronze, 17″ × 26″ × 49½″*

30 Heraldic Eagle, *marble, 17″ × 26″ × 49½″*

31 Praying Mantis, *onyx, 20″ × 11½″ × 30″*

32 Colt, Head Turned, *marble, 26″ × 9″ × 26″*

33 Colt, Head Turned, *golden bronze, 26″ × 9″ × 26″*

34 Colt, Head Turned, *bronze, 26″ × 9″ × 26″*

35 Hawk, *bronze, 16″ × 15″ × 14½″*

36 Hawk, *alabaster, 16″ × 15″ × 14½″*

37 Melanie (Desert Fox), *bronze, 10″ × 12″ × 4″*

38 Fennec, *bronze, 12½″ × 12½″ × 23½″*

39 La Nuit (detail), *marble, 51″ × 33½″ × 66½″*

40 La Nuit, *marble, 51″ × 33½″ × 66½″*

41 Mother and Son (detail), *granite, 22¾″ × 21½″ × 59″*

42 Mother and Son, *granite, 22¾″ × 21½″ × 59″*

43 Fallen Horse (study), *marble, 24″ × 7½″ × 13″*

44 Cobra, *bronze, 26″ × 31″ × 46″*

45 Giant Snail, *alabaster, 32″ × 16″ × 20″*

46 Snail, *alabaster, 21″ × 13″ × 14″*

47 Cobra, *alabaster, 26″ × 31″ × 46″*

48 Large Hawk, *bronze, 23″ × 14″ × 16″*

49 Hill Ponies, *alabaster, 9⅓″ × 12½″ × 33″*

50 Raven, *black granite, 23″ × 15″ × 17½″*

51 Large Swan, *alabaster, 26½″ × 26″ × 31½″*

52 Moon Dragons, *alabaster, 36″ × 24″ × 12½″*

53 Sea Hawk, *onyx, 11½″ × 7″ × 13½″*

54 Tibetan Pony, *bronze, 17″ × 7½″ × 10½″*

55 Bee, *alabaster, 17″ × 20½″ × 9″*

56 Tibetan Pony, *alabaster, 17″ × 7½″ × 10½″*

57 Europa (detail), *granite, 29″ × 22″ × 26″*

58 Europa, *bronze, 29″ × 22″ × 26″*

59 Europa (detail), *granite, 29″ × 22″ × 26″*

60 Eagle, *alabaster, 12½″ × 10″ × 13½″*

61 Eagle, *bronze, 12½″ × 10″ × 13½″*

62 Fallen Horse, *Volterra marble, 120″ × 40″ × 43½″*

63 Open Magnolia, *alabaster, 18½″ × 20″ × 12″*

64 Marmotte, *alabaster, 7⅔″ × 7″ × 19½″*

65 Marmotte, *bronze, 7⅔″ × 7″ × 19½″*

66 Owl Praying, *bronze, 7¾″ × 9½″ × 14*

67 Ghost Orchid, *alabaster, 9½″ × 6″ × 12½″*

68 Acanthe, *alabaster, 20″ × 14″ × 9½″*

69 Small Magnolia, *alabaster, 12¾″ × 10½″ × 6″*

70 Magnolia I, *alabaster, 18″ × 17″ × 13½″*

71 Rose, *red alabaster, 12″ × 9½″ × 5″*

72 Flamingo's Head, *bronze, 11″ × 9″ × 12″*

73 Woodcock, *bronze, 12″ × 12″ × 5″*

74 Tulip, *alabaster, 9″ × 9″ × 12¼″*

75 Bat, *red alabaster, 4″ × 14½″ × 10½″*

76 Fish IV, *alabaster, 10¾″ × 5½″ × 9″*

77 Tropical Flower, *alabaster, 20″ × 11½″ × 8¼″*

78 Quail, *golden bronze, 10½″ × 6½″ × 5¾″*

79 Mandarin Duck, *bronze, 10″ × 7″ × 6″*

80 White Sail, *alabaster, 11″ × 3¼″ × 16″*

81 Cheetah's Head, *bronze, 11″ × 8″ × 13″*

82 Giant Toad, *bronze, 11″ × 12″ × 11½″*

83 Mycenaean Bull's Head, *bronze, 13″ × 12″ × 12″*

84 Mountain Sheep, *dark bronze, 14″ × 15¾″ × 14″*

85 Ram's Head, *bronze, 11″ × 14″ × 20″*

86 Angry Owl, *bronze, 9″ × 10″ × 10½″*

87 Tree Frog II, *bronze, 10″ × 14″ × 5″*

88 Sweet Pea, *alabaster, 10″ × 20″ × 13½″*

89 Tree Frog II, *alabaster, 10″ × 14″ × 5″*

90 Tree Frog I, *soapstone, 10″ × 14″ × 5″*

91 Water Lily, *alabaster, 15″ × 16″ × 10″*

92 Anthurium III, *alabaster, 26″ × 16½″ × 14″*

93 Fish I, *alabaster, 14″ × 3½″ × 10″*

94 Fish I, *bronze, 14″ × 3½″ × 10″*

95 Hovering Owl, *bronze, 6½″ × 13½″ × 13″*

96 Dove Flying, *alabaster, 8″ × 4½″ × 9¼″*

97 Hovering Owl, *alabaster, 6½″ × 13½″ × 13″*

98 Lotus I, *alabaster, 12″ × 13″ × 7½″*

99 Lotus III, *alabaster, 12½″ × 10″ × 7½″*

100 Salamander, *alabaster, 12″ × 8″ × 4″*

101 Lotus Leaf, *marble, 14″ × 13″ × 2½″*

102 Salamander, *bronze, 12″ × 8″ × 4″*

103 Trillium, *alabaster, 18½″ × 16″ × 7″*

104 Swallow, *alabaster, 19½″ × 15″ × 8½″*

105 Swallow, *bronze, 19½″ × 15″ × 8½″*

106 Squirrel, *alabaster, 8″ × 6″ × 10″*

107 Sunflower, *alabaster, 15¼″ × 15½″ × 6″*

108 Rhododendron, *alabaster, 9″ × 9″ × 11½″*

109 Orchid, *alabaster, 14½″ × 12½″ × 6½″*

110 Monarch Butterfly, *alabaster, 22″ × 34½″ × 5″*

111 Iris, *alabaster, 17″ × 18″ × 20″*

112 Hibiscus, *alabaster, 15½″ × 16½″ × 8¾″*

113 Butterfly, *red alabaster, 10½″ × 1½″ × 7½″*

114 Photo Finish, *alabaster, 28″ × 18″ × 21″*

115 Photo Finish, *original alabaster and bronze cast, both 28″ × 18″ × 21″*

116 Jack in the Pulpit, *alabaster, 18½″ × 11″ × 11″*

117 Closed Tulip, *alabaster, 8¼″ × 8¼″ × 9½″*

118 Sparrow Hawk, *soapstone, 5″ × 4″ × 10″*

119 Baby Seal, *alabaster, 16½″ × 7½″ × 5″*

120 Poppy, *alabaster, 15″ × 15½″ × 4½″*

121 Bali Bird, *bronze, 18″ × 6″ × 5½″*

122 Snowbird, *alabaster, 13″ × 11½″ × 11½″*

123 Red Rose, *red alabaster, 8⅓″ × 6½″ × 5″*

124 Moth, *pink alabaster, 7″ × 2″ × 9½″*

125 Snake, *soapstone, 14″ × 9″ × 3″*

126 The Wave, *alabaster, 28″ × 15″ × 13″*

127 Anthurium I, *alabaster, 17″ × 15″ × 9″*

128 Dranunculas Vulgaris, *pink alabaster, 7″ × 8½″ × 22″*

129 Oriental Goldfish, *alabaster, 12″ × 5½″ × 7½″*

130 Fish III, *bronze, 9″ × 4¼″ × 6¼″*

131 Anthurium II, *alabaster, 20″ × 13″ × 8″*

132 Mare and Foal, *alabaster, 19½″ × 15″ × 12″*

133 Mare and Foal, *alabaster, 19½″ × 15″ × 12″*

EXHIBITIONS

Galerie Hervé, Paris, 1962
Rotapfel-Galerie, Zurich, 1965
O'Hana Gallery, London, 1965
La Demeure, Paris, 1973
Palm Beach Galleries, Palm Beach, 1974
Bodley Gallery, New York, 1975
The Saratoga Gallery, Saratoga Springs, New York, 1976
Kenneth Neame, London, 1979
Galerie du Bost, Paris, 1980
Seaview Gallery, Palm Beach, 1980
Old Westbury Gardens, Old Westbury, New York, 1981
First National, Palm Beach, 1987
Phipps Conservatory, Pittsburgh, 1987
The Governor's Club, Palm Beach, 1989
Brooklyn Botanic Garden, Brooklyn, 1990

SALONS

Salon d'Automne, Paris, 1961
Salon de Femmes Peintres et Sculpteurs, Formes Humaines, Paris, 1965
Salon International, Paris, 1967
Salon Femmes Peintres et Sculpteurs, Istanbul, 1967
Floralis d'Orleans, Formes Humaines, Paris, 1968
Salon International Art Contemporain Musée Rodin, Paris, 1970
Formes Humaines, Musée Rodin, Paris, 1975
Musée du Luxembourg, Paris, 1976
Formes Humaines, Musée Rodin, Paris, 1977
Formes Humaines, Musée Rodin, Paris, 1979
La Galerie de l'Esplanade à la Défense, Paris, 1982

Jacket design by Russell Chatham and Anne Garner.
Set in Bembo and Centaur types by Wilsted & Taylor, Oakland.
Printed and bound at the Stinehour Press, Lunenburg, Vermont.

Grateful acknowledgment is made to Salomé Vernard,
Guayo de Leon, Vincent Delmotte,
Guy de la Valdène, Lorraine Odasso,
Russell Chatham, Stacy Feldmann,
and Jamie Potenberg.

Diana Guest, born in England, began her career as a sculptor in the fifties, and since then her work has been exhibited at galleries in Paris, London, Switzerland and New York, as well as at the Brooklyn Botanical Gardens and the Phipps Conservatory in Pittsburgh. She divides her time between Palm Beach, Florida, and Normandy, France.